Understanding World Religions *in Early Years Practice*

Jennie Lindon

HODDER
EDUCATION
UK

Dedication

To Lance, Tanith and Drew

Orders: please contact Bookpoint Ltd, 130 Milton Park, Abingdon, Oxon OX14 4SB, UK. Telephone: (44) 01235 827720, Fax: (44) 01235 400454. Lines are open from 9.00—5.00, Monday to Saturday, with a 24 hour message answering service. You can also order through our website: www.hoddereducation.co.uk

British Library Cataloguing in Publication Data
A catalogue record for this title is available from The British Library

ISBN 978 0 340 74786 5

First published 1999
Impression number   10   9   8
Year   2009   2008

Cover illustrated by Gill Sampson
Typeset by Wearset, Boldon, Tyne and Wear.
Printed in India for Hodder Education, part of Hachette Livre UK,
338 Euston Road, London NW1 3BH by Replika Press Pvt. Ltd.

Contents

Acknowledgements   v
Introduction   vi

Chapter 1   Religion, culture and society   1
- Introduction   1
- Understanding the significance of religious faith   1
- A practical note on dates and spelling   8

Chapter 2   World faiths I   11
- Introduction   11
- Judaism   11
- Christianity   17
- Islam   26

Chapter 3   World faiths II   34
- Introduction   34
- Hinduism   34
- Buddhism   41
- Sikhism   48

Chapter 4   Philosophical and faith belief systems   59
- Introduction   59
- Humanism   59
- Existentialism   61
- New Age movements   64

Chapter 5   A focus on children's development   75
- Introduction   75
- Children's development as a whole   75
- Children's communicative and intellectual development   77
- Children's moral development   81
- Children's spiritual and personal development   88

Chapter 6 Legal requirements, policy and practice   98
- Introduction   98
- Working with children in schools   98

- Education in Scotland 105
- Education in Northern Ireland 106
- Working with children in the early years and playwork 107
- The UN Convention on the Rights of the Child 112
- Development of a policy 113
- Key issues in good practice 116
- Partnership with parents 119

Chapter 7   Exploring festivals with children 123
- Introduction 123
- Why celebrate festivals? 123
- Festivals from six world faiths 129
- Common themes in the celebration of festivals 150

Chapter 8   Supporting children's learning 155
- Introduction 155
- Using books and story-telling 155
- Taking children on visits 161
- Learning about religious artefacts 164
- Broad learning from RE 165
- Applications of faith to everyday living 170

Chapter 9   Overview 178
- Some thoughts on good practice 178

Appendix 1 180
- Further resources 180

Appendix 2 182
- Links to qualifications 182

Index 183

Acknowledgements

Over the years I have enjoyed and learned from many conversations with colleagues, early years workers, parents and children. Such conversations have been invaluable in helping me to see beyond my own perspective, and disagreements have been equally as useful as agreements.

I would especially like to thank the following people for their help as I wrote this book. Tanith Lindon and Nick Katz for letting me read their school coursework on religious education. Ann Douglas (Head) and Helen McAuley (Deputy Head) of the Balham Nursery School for sharing their approach to celebrations and their moral and spiritual policy. Sue Westfold (Wandsworth Adult College) for her experience in playgroups. Tess Robson (Head of Tachbrook Nursery School) for discussing policy and practice. Lance Lindon for his knowledge of astrology and some of the ancient crafts within New Age movements. Drew Lindon for help on the sociology of religion. Ann Robinson (Information Officer, Early Childhood Unit) for her invaluable reading lists and for finding articles for me. Alison Seaman (Director of the National Society RE Centre) and Geoff Teece (Director of Westhill RE Centre) for help with policy and practice in RE syllabuses for England and Wales. Kevin Kelman (Glasgow College) for information on the teaching of RE in Scotland. Siobhan Fitzgerald (Director of NIPPA), Ruth Sinclair (Research Director, National Children's Bureau), Bob Hughes (PlayEducation UK) and Chris Tracey (Council for the Curriculum Examinations and Assessment) for explaining early years practice and RE in Northern Ireland. Finally, thank you to Lance, who took most of the photographs in the book and to the children and staff of Balham Nursery School and Ravenstone Primary School.

Introduction

The context of this book

Religious faith is of great and direct importance in some people's lives. It also plays an underestimated role in the lives of many more, for whom a dominant religion has shaped their cultural background. In the case of Britain, this has been the Christian faith.

A positive approach to understanding religious belief is part of good practice in work with children in all different care, educational and playwork settings. There are obligations to be met, but also a range of ways that workers can meet them and respond properly to the faiths and concerns of the local population. However, many workers and advisors are uncertain how to approach this area, wary of the possible pitfalls and uneasy about a suitable balance between personal commitment and an open approach to children's learning.

Within the framework of legislation and guidance, it is crucial that nobody loses sight of the children. We need to keep in mind what children are likely to understand and be able to learn at different ages and stages. It is also vital that adults try to remember what it is like to be a child. Children have a refreshing capacity for seeing through simplistic adult reasoning, pious hopes and one-way rule systems.

It is important that adults talk with each other, not least because the topic of religious, spiritual and moral development concerns many people and covers such a range of highly diverse views. However, the end result will not promote children's understanding unless everyone recalls that children are in the process of developing and need to learn step-by-step.

In writing this book I was constantly reminded of the great variety within, as well as between, major world faiths. I also needed to recognise the equally heartfelt views of people who take a Humanist approach or who have become involved in one of the New Age movements. Wherever possible I have drawn on two or preferably three different sources of information when writing the chapters about different faiths and the background to their celebrations. In a book of this length it was inappropriate to explore the many divisions, and arguments, within most world faiths. I have, nevertheless, tried to avoid an implication of greater agreement than is the case. Of course, I take responsibility for any mistakes or misunderstandings on my part and hope that readers will take the time to alert me to these. I will be only too pleased to modify future editions.

Aims of the book

This book is divided into two parts. Chapters 1–4 focus on information about world religious and philosophical beliefs and practice, whereas Chapters 5–9 focus on good practice with children. The book as a whole has several aims, which are to:

- Encourage you to learn about world faiths, to extend your knowledge and to provoke your interest in finding out more.
- Motivate you to stand back from your own beliefs, whether religious or **secular** (non-religious), and to inspire you to learn with an open mind about the beliefs and practices of other people.
- Promote respect for other adults and their beliefs, whilst recognising that you have a right to your own perspective, so long as you do not impose this on others.
- Focus on children, their development and capacity for learning, and to support you in developmentally appropriate practice with them.
- Help you to understand your obligations in this area within the law and expectations of good practice, including those areas in which you and your colleagues will have to make your own decisions.
- Provide a resource of information and ideas for how you can appropriately work with children.
- Help you to be honest and straightforward with children, both in terms of the information and understanding that you offer them, and in a full respect for their developing beliefs and attitudes.

1

Religion, culture and society

Introduction

Most, possibly all, the societies that exist and have existed in the world have contained some elements of religious faith. The predominant religion or religions have sometimes been central to the way in which a society is organised and run. Sometimes religions have been more a matter of personal and family practice. This first part of the book concentrates on six major and current world faiths and some relatively recent movements. However, the sum total of religious belief and practice within the history of humankind is considerably more extensive than the scope of this book.

Understanding the significance of religious faith

Ancient societies from pre-history frequently show evidence, for instance from archaeological exploration, of a concern with spiritual matters and ritual. Making meaning from archaeological treasures is fraught with difficulty, since the assumptions and priorities of those ancient societies may have been very different from the social experience of the men and women who dig up these artefacts. Anthropological studies of societies relatively untouched by outside influences also show evidence of spiritual beliefs and practices that guide the society. Again, objective and even-handed study can be undermined by the researchers' assumptions and by dismissive attitudes that divide religious faiths into those which are deemed to be more sophisticated and the so-called 'primitive' religions.

Meeting human needs

RELIGIOUS FAITH

There seem to be a number of basic human needs that have often been met by religious faith of different kinds.

- People, ancient and modern, have sought a sense of meaning and purpose for daily life and personal choices. Over the centuries people have searched for answers to significant questions of existence –

> Why are we here?
>
> What is the point of our lives?
>
> Why do some people have significantly harder and more tragic lives than others?
>
> What happens after bodily death?

- People seek greater certainty and predictability of the obvious, and sometimes disturbing, uncertainties of life –

  > Why do certain events happen, especially tragedies and personal loss?
  >
  > Can humans influence matters at all?

- People sometimes seek a 'guarantee' that they can direct their own lives, that their actions will have some predictable outcome now, or in an after life.

- On the other hand, religious belief has sometimes been part of the search for ways to influence the natural world and to control events. A sense of control has been especially important to societies, ancient and more recent, for whom the vagaries of weather can mean the difference between living and dying, because of the effects on the food supply or because of the threat of a natural disaster.

- People require ways to guide and rules to structure daily living, and to be sure that these ways are more right than wrong. Issues of common concern are diet, dress, family life and how to raise children. Guidance and a level of certainty may also be sought for other social relationships and hierarchies within a given society.

- People need a focus for celebrations and rituals for the important events in life and for bringing people together. Such shared activities meet the need for a positive feeling of identity, the answer to the questions 'Who am I?' and 'With whom can I feel a sense of belonging?'

- People look for a way to interpret phenomena that are not easily explained by rational means or human experience to date. Humans seek explanations both for unusual natural phenomena and the internal experience of dreams.

POLITICAL MOVEMENTS

These human needs have often been met through religious commitment, but this option is not the only way. Studies of powerful political movements frequently show that they offer their members certainty in a world that is essentially uncertain. Strong political commitment can also offer a source of identity, created both by a sense of belonging and by being clearly divided from rival groups. Political philosophies often provide a guide, sometimes very rigid, on how to behave towards others, make choices and organise priorities. For a good example of how political movements can meet human needs, you could read *Wild Swans* by Jung Chang (Harper Collins, 1991) a description of growing up and early adulthood in Maoist China.

Diversity within world religions

The history and current practice of all the major world faiths show variations within the worldwide religious community. There is no main world faith of which you can you confidently say 'everyone believes that…' or 'everyone behaves in this way'. You are probably more aware of the variety of beliefs and sub-groups within the world faith that you know best, but diversity is a feature of every significant faith. There is nothing like complete agreement on key beliefs, interpretations of the main holy book or books, the details of everyday practice like diet and dress or on many other aspects of religious activity and related cultural tradition.

THE IMPACT OF HUMAN NATURE

Human nature is at the root of at least some of the immense diversity. It seems that humans cannot be long in a group, especially one fuelled by strong religious or political beliefs, before there are arguments and consequent schisms. The Christian faith, for example, has a vast array of sub-groups, confusing even for those within the faith, let alone to non-Christians. Some of the different groups are very large, although some are numerically small. Many have broken away on a point of principle: the interpretation of religious dogma, questions of ultimate authority or disagreements about the authenticity of a new charismatic leader. Other world faiths, described in Chapters 2 and 3, also have many different groupings.

Human beings, inspired by religious, political or philosophical fervour and conviction can be capable of acts of great kindness and selflessness. Unfortunately, they are equally capable of heart stopping cruelty, especially once they have rejected another social or ethnic group for their beliefs, even when those beliefs can seem very similar to an outsider. Some of the religious arguments have historically led to violence and oppression, within a given faith as well as between faiths. For instance, some Protestant and Puritan groups, who emigrated to the east coast of what became the United States of America, had left Europe largely because of religious persecution. They then proceeded to split into sub-groups and, in some cases, started to persecute those who challenged the official religious line in the same way they had been attacked previously.

THE SPREAD OF A FAITH

A second important reason for diversity within the faiths is that all the major world religions have spread further than the country or community in which they started. Individuals and families who emigrated established their faith in their new home countries and, in some cases, differences in practice developed over the years. Some religions have been actively promoted through evangelical work: practitioners of the faith deliberately set out to convert people in other cultures. Over time, some religions developed significant variations in their different locations.

Some religions changed as they deliberately absorbed the practices of pre-existing religions in the new culture. For instance, Buddhism in India differs from Japanese Buddhism. The latter developed in coexistence with Shintoism, an ancient religion based in **animist beliefs** of a supernatural force within all natural objects.

Geographical distance probably enhanced divergence of faiths, especially since easy travel and communications are recent inventions. Some variations arose from unresolved arguments over doctrine within the faith and separate religious communities taking a different spiritual direction over time. For instance, the Orthodox Church in Eastern Europe split permanently from the Western European Church in around 1054. The unresolved schism arose mainly from arguments about the nature of the Trinity (see page 19) and the authority of the Pope in Rome. The Western Church later split into Protestant and Catholic Christianity, fuelled in part by the marital and political problems of King Henry VIII of England.

DIVERSITY IN PRACTICE

This book does not attempt to cover all the differences and arguments within the main world faiths. (If you want to explore variations, try the further reading suggested on page 56.) In terms of application to work with children, you are not expected to develop an extensive knowledge of all the variations within the main world faiths. *However, it is important to be aware that such diversity exists.* In your practice, this could make the simple difference between saying, 'All Hindus believe that . . .' and, 'Many Hindus believe that . . .'. It would be poor practice if the way that you presented religious faiths and daily life to the children implied that people from a less familiar group were 'all the same' while a more familiar group was shown with variety.

Some believers, within what appears to outsiders to be the same faith, disagree strongly over doctrine or daily practice. It is possible that disagreements in your local community may spill over into your setting, especially if you work with older children in a primary school or an after-school club. Children who are aware of divisions between adults often express similar arguments between themselves or reject other children on the basis of their family's particular religious allegiance. If you work in Northern Ireland, for instance, you will be only too aware of the very young age at which children learn the fierce divisions between the two Christian communities of Protestant and Catholic.

Religion embedded in the culture

Religious beliefs and practices have shaped many societies worldwide. When a particular faith has been part of a society for a long time, the religious practices often become intermingled with the culture to form **traditions** that affect virtually every aspect of that society: social, moral and political. The traditions originated with specific beliefs in the religious faith but then become part of what people see as 'normal' life. Simplified religious ideas are absorbed into everyday language and rituals, and religious celebrations continue but with secular cultural overtones rather than religious ones.

An awareness of how religious and cultural tradition can merge is relevant to your work with children and families. For instance, parents may make a request about diet for their child, but from their conversation you may realise that the family is not actively involved in the religious faith. It is good practice to follow and respect the parents' request – do not consider overlooking it on the grounds that these parents are 'not serious'. Adults raised in a faith such as Islam or Judaism, which provides clear direction about permitted and forbidden foods, often feel uncomfortable about breaking the rules they learned as children.

RELIGION IN ENGLAND, SCOTLAND AND WALES

English society has a long history of being shaped by Christianity and this historical fact is acknowledged in the guidance on the approach to religions in the school curriculum. The Church of England is the established church and for a long time being 'C of E' was regarded by many people as much the same as being 'English'. For instance, people would give this description on any forms asking for their religion, whether or not they were regular church attenders. It is only in relatively recent years that it has become more usual to refer to someone's *personal name* rather than their 'Christian' name: a link with the religious practice and cultural habit of christening babies.

Of course, there were, and still are, different groups within Christianity and England is not the only country in Britain. Neither Welsh Methodists nor

Scottish Presbyterians would appreciate being merged with the English version of Christianity, especially since such groups have an important history of marking their differences from the Church of England.

•••••••••••••••••••••• *To think about* ••••••••••••••••••••••

During November 1997 the Archbishop of Canterbury, George Carey, made public his disagreement with the promotion of inter-faith worship in Britain. He supported his view by claiming, 'Other faiths comprise less than 10% of the population. So, 90% are still rooted in a Christian position.' (in an interview for the magazine *Third Way*).

Of course, considerably less than 90% of the population are regular church attenders or profess an active commitment to the Christian faith. However, with the historical predominance of Christianity in British society, Dr Carey felt justified to count as nominally Christian anyone in Britain who had not actively committed to another faith.

Comments

You may find this attitude reflected by members of your own team, or by volunteers in your setting, until such views are openly discussed. For instance, perhaps someone says of a family, 'Oh, they're just normal C of E' or tries to add 'Christian' to the written record of a white child when the parents have left the space blank.

- In an open-minded way, listen out for any similar assumptions expressed within your team or in your course group as a student.
- Be ready to discuss the assumptions underlying any such remark. Make your conversation *constructive*, not critical of the person who expressed the view.

Increased secularisation of society

Religious faith is still very important for a considerable number of people around the world. However, Western societies have experienced a change described as the **secularisation** of society, meaning that there has been a long-term decline in the influence of religion, specifically Christianity, on national life. Secular priorities have become more important for many people than, for example, the values and rules of the previously dominant Church of England (the official and established Church in Britain). Sociologists who study religion in society do not all agree that there has been a widespread secularisation – some suggest that a more accurate view is that spiritual beliefs and human needs are addressed in different ways.

SCIENTIFIC AND RATIONAL EXPLANATIONS

For many centuries, some discoveries of science have been incompatible with, or created serious difficulties for, religious beliefs. For instance, the growth of theories of evolution directly challenged the creation story as believed by Christians and described in the Old Testament. This argument continues as some committed Christians reject evolution theory in favour of creationist explanations. In the USA, parents' groups have sometimes succeeded in removing any discussion of evolution from their local school curriculum. Sometimes, science has created the possibility of procedures and actions that bring about ethical dilemmas, for example with *in vitro* fertilisation and related research on human embryos. These situations may be a challenge to prevailing religious doctrine, but ethical concerns are not *only* the preserve of members of established faiths. Scientific discovery seems to encourage a more secular view by having a rational explanation for everything. However, some scientists find their profession to be compatible with their religious faith and, for many people, scientific discovery does not impinge on their beliefs one way or another.

USE OF RELIGIOUS SERVICES

Christian faith as shown by attendance at mainstream churches in Britiain has declined. However, many people who do not attend formal worship still claim to have some personal beliefs of a spiritual nature. Christianity has become such a part of the social fabric that people who do not attend any services nevertheless often still expect to be able to be married in their local church, to have babies christened and to have a funeral service for members of their family. There is still a sense for many people that these are the right ways to handle significant life events.

MATERIALISM

The secularisation of society has also been linked to an increased emphasis on material goods and a lifestyle of conspicuous consumption. There is good reason to argue that some Christian religious celebrations, notably Christmas and to an extent Easter, have been taken over as commercial opportunities. Over recent decades there has also been a great increase in lifestyle books and magazine articles, which offer guidance on how to behave and run one's life but which do not draw on religious precepts at all. In addition, members of some mainstream religious faiths have also demonstrated a love of materialism and conspicuous show. Some forms of Puritan Christianity have specifically linked material success with godliness, for example.

SUPPORT FOR NON-CHRISTIAN FAITHS

The argument that Britain has become mainly a secular society tends to count Christianity as the only faith of any importance. Britain is now a multi-cultural and multi-faith society and a proportion of the population are committed members of world faiths other than Christianity. Since the 1960s, there has also been an upsurge of interest in broader spiritual ideas, particularly through the varied New Age movements.

ALTERNATIVE WAYS OF MEETING HUMAN NEEDS

Some people with a loosely Christian background still look towards their parish church for weddings and funerals. However, it is possible to meet a shared human wish for ritual and celebration through ways outside conventional religious ceremony (see the box on page 9).

A practical note on dates and spelling

Calendars and dates

The Western system of months and years is based on the movement of the sun (a **solar calendar**) and its historical origin is linked with a solar-based system of astrology. But many other parts of the world use a system based on the movements of the moon (a **lunar calendar**) and astrology in the Far East is a lunar system.

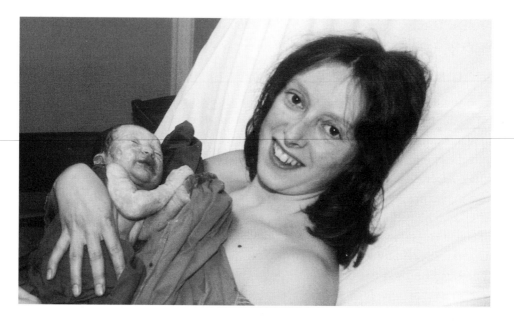

People usually want to mark important life events

• **To think about** •

Many people wish to have a special event to mark significant milestones or changes in their lives and to bring friends and family together at such times. The British Humanist Association has responded to this need by training people to help to arrange and to officiate at non-religious ceremonies to celebrate marriages, welcoming or naming ceremonies for babies and funeral services.

- You might like to consider, and discuss with colleagues, this human need to mark special occasions. What do you think we all gain from such ceremonies?

When ritual disappears, people sometimes feel at a loss and wish to mark their feelings in some way. During the 1980s and 90s a new cultural tradition developed of placing flowers at the location of a fatal road accident or other tragedy. (This secular ritual was well established years before its most public use after the death of Diana, Princess of Wales in 1997.)

- What do you think may be people's reasons for placing flowers at the site of a tragedy or in some cases outside the home of a bereaved family?

The lunar calendar is shorter than the solar one by about 11 days, so the dates of festivals based on a lunar calendar move in relation to the solar calendar. Important religious dates or festivals, with which you are unfamiliar, are *not* moving at random. Dates are determined in a predictable way, if you know the underlying system. Workers with a Christian background often express surprise at the apparently changing dates, but this assumption arises only because Christmas is the same date each year.

Years

The tradition of dating familiar in Britain depends on taking an arbitrary zero for the year estimated for the birth of Jesus Christ. Years are then counted backwards from that point labelled BC (Before Christ) and forwards for years labelled as AD (Anno Domini, which is Latin for 'In the year of our Lord'). This system has continued since it is well established within cultures influenced by Christianity, although more recent historical evidence suggests that Christ was born at least four years and possibly seven years earlier than the zero point. The terms AD and BC now tend to be replaced by CE (common era) and BCE (before common era) as a more accurate reflection of the arbitrary nature of the dating and to reflect a multi-faith society. I have followed this newer tradition when I give dates.

Other faiths and the cultures influenced by them, not surprisingly, have different year dating systems. For instance, the Jewish calendar is counted from what is 3761 BCE in the Western calendar, because Jews believe that this is the year in which the world was created. In discussing different faiths and festivals I have given dates in the Christian European style calendar, but these *will not necessarily* be the same as that used by the faith.

Spelling

One further practical area of difference arises over spelling. The world religions covered in this book originated and are practised in countries that do not share the same language, written script or alphabet. Decisions about how to translate and spell religious terms have therefore led to variations. The Hindu and Sikh festival of Divali also appears as Diwali. The Jewish festival of Hanukkah can be spelled as Chanukah. For consistency I have followed wherever possible the spelling given for religious terms in *Religious education: glossary of terms,* published by the School Curriculum and Assessment Authority in 1994. This glossary was produced in consultation with all the relevant faith communities. I have only deviated from the glossary pattern when I recommend a book in which the title uses a different spelling.

In summary

You need to understand the significance of religious belief and practice within society and be able to consider the intellectual, spiritual, emotional and moral human needs that, for some people, are met through their faith. Your role will be to respond positively to children's individual identity as shaped by the faith of their family. Your task is also to help all the children in your care to understand the perspectives of different groups within society and to value such differences day by day in your setting. You *can* extend understanding without promoting a specific faith. Furthermore, respect can be encouraged, without requiring an inappropriate reverence.

In order to work well with children and their families, you will need to extend your own knowledge and understanding. Chapters 1–4 of this book provides information and suggestions for finding out more. Chapters 5–9 address the details of practice with children in early years, educational and playwork settings.

2

World Faiths I: Judaism, Christianity, Islam

Introduction

Judaism, Christianity and Islam are three world faiths with some common ground historically and this is the reason that I have placed them together in this chapter. They are all **monotheistic faiths**: followers believe in one god. However, beliefs and religious practice are distinct between the faiths and all three have divisions within the faith. As you read both this chapter and Chapter 3, it is very important to bear in mind that there is variety in all the main world faiths. In this chapter and Chapter 3, I have described the lives of important figures within a faith using the details commonly accepted by believers. In all instances, it is difficult to distinguish between those parts which have some historical basis and those which are hard to prove one way or another. I have not attempted to make any such distinction.

Judaism

Historical background and key beliefs

Judaism has existed as a faith for about 3500 years and is the first religion known to be monotheistic. Judaism started in what is now the Middle East. Jewish populations are now distributed around the world but they regard Israel as their homeland. The modern Jewish State of Israel was founded in 1948 within the larger area of what was previously known as Palestine.

Jews believe in one God who created the world and everything in it. They believe that the Jewish people were chosen to be an example to all humankind and that God delivered the original Jews, the Israelites, out of slavery in Egypt and, through leaders like Moses and Joshua, led them to the Holy or Promised Land. This area was called the land of Canaan and the Jewish people began to refer to it as Israel. They believe that God communicated a moral code through the prophets and that this guidance is set out in the Torah (see below). Jews believe that we have only one life and that our obligation is to obey God's laws within that life. Judaism recognises an afterlife but is mainly concerned about followers' behaviour in this life.

Writings and holy books

Jewish scriptures were written over a period of nearly 1000 years and were established in their final form by about the end of the first century CE. In essence, the holy books are a record of the aspirations of Jewish people to understand God in relation to the material world and to humanity.

The collection of 24 books of the Jewish scriptures is called the **Tenakh** and comprises three sections: the **Torah**, **Nevi'im** (meaning prophets) and **Ketuvim** (meaning writings**)**.

The Torah (meaning law or teaching) includes the five books of Moses. (These are the first five books of what Christians call the **Old Testament**.) Orthodox Jews aim to follow in detail all the requirements of the Torah, whereas other Jewish groups, for instance Reform Jews, believe that the guidance is open to interpretation for life in a changing society. The laws covered by the Torah include the **Ten Commandments**, believed (by Jews and Christians) to have been given by God to the prophet Moses in the form of tablets of stone. The Torah is in **Hebrew**, an ancient Semitic language also used for prayer and study. (The Semites were the dominant ethnic group in what is now known as the Middle East in the centuries that passed BCE. The word 'Semitic' is now more often used just to mean 'Jewish'.) Modern Hebrew as spoken in Israel has many differences. Some religious terms are in **Yiddish**, a common language form which is a mixture of German, Russian and Hebrew.

The Nevi'im contains the stories of the lives of prophets such as Elijah and Isaiah. The Ketuvim includes examples of holy writings such as psalms and proverbs. (These books are also within what Christians call the Old Testament.)

The **Talmud** is a substantial collection of the teachings of Rabbis. The Talmud comprises the **Mishnah**, the first written form of Jewish oral tradition (written in about 200 CE) and the **Gemara**, a series of commentaries on the teachings.

Worship

Jews worship in the **Synagogue**, a building for public prayer, study and assembly. Services in some synagogues are led by the **Chazan** (or cantor). A

Rabbi is an ordained Jewish teacher, who is often also the local religious leader. Rabbis instruct the congregation in the faith and make decisions over Jewish legal questions. Synagogues for Orthodox Jews seat males separately from females, whereas Reform groups have mixed congregations and have ordained female Rabbis.

Jews worship through prayer as a means to realise a relationship with God and to be open to positive influence. The most important Jewish prayer is contained in the **Shema**, three passages from the Torah which are read every morning and evening by devout Jews and which affirm their belief in God. For weekday morning prayers Jewish men wear **tefillin**, which are small leather boxes containing passages from the Torah and which are strapped to the forehead and arm. A **mezuzah** is fixed to the doorposts of devout Jewish homes. This is a scroll that contains a section from the Torah and is sometimes enclosed in a decorative case. As people enter the home, they touch the mezuzah and place their fingers to their lips as a reminder of the love that God has for the Jewish people.

Jews believe that the sacred name of God was revealed to Moses but that it should not be spoken. Non-Jews may refer to Yahweh or Jehovah as the God of Jewish faith, but Jews do not speak in this way.

Shabbat (sometimes called the Sabbath by non-Jews) is the most important holy day each week and lasts for 25 hours from sunset on Friday evening until the stars shine in the night sky on Saturday. Shabbat is celebrated through worship in the Synagogue but specific events within the family are equally important. Shabbat preparations include cleaning the home, putting on fresh clothes, blessings and prayers and a family meal. Shabbat is welcomed each week by the women in the family lighting two special candles and saying a special blessing. This is followed by the **Kiddush**, a blessing pronounced by the male head of the household over bread and wine. The family then sit down to the first of three special meals to be eaten over the Shabbat period.

Shabbat is a time of prayer and worship and symbolises the final day of the week in which God is believed to have created the world: on the seventh day God rested. Consequently, Jews who follow the rules in full will avoid any kind of work, paid or domestic. They avoid journeys that cannot be taken on foot and avoid use of modern technology and appliances. This is so that Jews can approach Shabbat as a day of rest and spiritual renewal, to be spent with the family, in worship at the Synagogue and in visiting friends nearby.

Rituals

Naming and initiation ceremonies

Babies are brought into the Jewish community through the **Brit Milah** (circumcision) ceremony for baby boys when they are eight days old. Baby girls are taken to the Synagogue for a naming ceremony on the first Shabbat after birth. A girl's father is called to the **bimah** (the raised platform from which the Torah is read) and his daughter's name is announced to the congregation.

At 13 years a boy is judged to pass into manhood and become **Bar Mitzvah**, meaning Son of Commandment. Boys' coming of age is prepared by study of the Torah, and learning Hebrew, if he does not already speak the language. Boys attend a ceremony in the Synagogue on the first Shabbat after their twelfth birthday at which they read from the Torah during the service and wear their **tallit** (prayer shawl) for the first time. Families usually have a celebration or party afterwards. Girls come of age at 12 years old and become **Bat Mitzvah** (Daughter of Commandment). This event is marked differently between Jewish communities; some Synagogues hold a ceremony for girls.

Weddings

Marriages are celebrated in a wedding service and usually take place on a Sunday. Some Jewish groups prefer to arrange the marriages of their sons and daughters. On the Shabbat before the wedding the groom goes to the Synagogue and reads from the Torah. The groom is traditionally dressed in dark colours and the bride in white. They stand under a **huppah** (canopy) which represents their future home and happiness. The Rabbi pours wine and the marriage contract is read. The groom places a plain gold ring on the first finger of the bride's left hand, tells everyone that she is his bride and then moves the ring to the third finger. There is a second cup of wine and the Rabbi says seven blessings, which praise God and ask for happiness for the couple. At the end of ceremony the groom breaks a small glass with his foot (symbolic of the destruction of the temple at Jerusalem) and the congregation call out 'mazel tov' (congratulations).

•••••••••••••••••••••• *Arranged marriages* ••••••••••••••••••••

Comment

British cultural tradition does not usually include arranged marriages, and such traditions are often misunderstood. A number of world faiths are part of cultural traditions in which the marriage of two people is seen as a bringing together of families and not just the individuals' life choice. If the young couple are to live under the same roof as the rest of the extended family, some degree of compatibility can be especially important.

In many cases (not only in Judaism) the young people themselves are part of the discussion to decide on the shortlist of potential partners and they have a substantial say in the final choice. Some families who arrange marriages behave in an authoritarian way with their sons or daughters. However, such pressure is certainly not an inevitable part of the process and young people can be bullied in families from any cultural or religious background. Misunderstandings about the arranged marriage system has led some people to prefer the term 'assisted marriages'.

Funerals

Funeral services are kept simple and should be held within 24 hours of death. Orthodox Jews bury their dead, whereas Progressive Jews may cremate. It is the special responsibility of a son to say **Kaddish**, a prayer of praise to God in the memory of a deceased parent. In the absence of a son, another male relative or friend will say the prayer. There is also a tradition of keeping two lighted candles on the graves of women to recall the candles that they light to begin Shabbat.

Celebrations

As well as worship at the Synagogue, the Jewish family home is a very important focus for religious observance and the celebration of key festivals within the Jewish year. Some of the main festivals include:

- **Purim** – this happens in February or March and celebrates the historical story of the deliverance of the Jews from persecution in what was then Persia. The day is celebrated with a great deal of fun, including fancy dress. (See also page 134.)
- **Pesach** (or **Passover**) – this happens in March or April and marks the safe deliverance of the Jews from slavery in Egypt in about 1300 BCE. The festival lasts for eight days. The first two and last two days are especially holy and Jewish children do not attend school. On the eve of Pesach families take part in an important ceremonial meal at home, called the

Seder and the story of the exodus from Egypt is told from a special book, the **Hagadah**. (See also page 135.)

- **Rosh Hashanah** is the Jewish New Year and falls in September or October. With Yom Kippur (see below), this is one of the two most important festivals in the Jewish Year. Rosh Hashanah celebrates both the creation of the world and the start of the new year. Over these two days, Jewish people believe that they are symbolically judged by God. The **Shofar**, a ram's horn, is blown as a call for repentance. Children do not attend school on these days and join their families to attend Synagogue.

- **Yom Kippur** is the **Day of Atonement** and falls ten days after Rosh Hashanah. Yom Kippur is a day of fasting from the evening before to nightfall on the day. Many Jewish people remain in the Synagogue throughout the day in worship and quiet contemplation. This activity is a continuation of the penitence and asking for forgiveness that started in the new year. By the end of the day, Jewish people feel that they have been spiritually reborn to start afresh.

- **Hanukkah** falls in November or December and marks the recovery of the temple at Jerusalem after its destruction by Syrian invaders some 2000 years ago. The festival is a family celebration to recall this part of the shared history of the Jewish people. (See also page 136.)

Symbols

An important Jewish symbol is the **Magen David** (meaning the Shield of David) and popularly known as the **Star of David**. Another common symbol is the seven-branched candelabrum, the **Menorah**, which is lit daily in the temple.

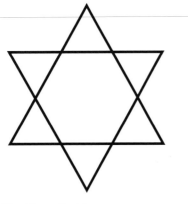

The Magen David

The Menorah

Application to daily life

DIET

The laws of **Kashrut** determine which foods can be eaten and those that are forbidden, the method of slaughter of animals and the preparation of food. Permitted foods (**Kosher**, meaning fit or proper) include animals with a cloven hoof, birds that are not predators and fish with fins. Meat and poultry must be obtained from Kosher butchers because animals have to be slaughtered in such a way that all the blood drains out of the bodies. The meat is then blessed by the Rabbi. Meat and dairy products should be kept completely separate at all stages of food preparation, serving and eating and in washing up afterwards.

In neighbourhoods with a large number of Jewish families you will see notices in the windows of some food shops and restaurants to show that these establishments are accredited by the local religious body and follow all the requirements of Kashrut.

Fasting and some limitations on normal diet are important for several Jewish celebrations. For instance, people fast for the 25 hours of Yom Kippur and avoid yeast-based products during Pesach.

CLOTHING

Some stricter Jewish groups require women to cover their hair at all times. Boys and men wear a **kippah** (a skull cap covering part of the head) at prayer and some wear it all the time.

Christianity

Background

Christians share a belief in one God who created the world and in the human form of God in **Jesus Christ** (the Messiah). He was born to a Jewish family and lived in Palestine about 2000 years ago, at a time when the country was occupied by Romans.

Jesus was born in Bethlehem, part of Judea, but he was raised in Galilee (all of which were areas of what was then known as Palestine). His family were respectable, although not affluent, and his father Joseph was a general builder, an important job in village life. The Jewish people were resentful of the Roman rule and revolts were relatively common. Jews had long expected to be saved through the arrival of a messiah, who would not only bring spiritual enrichment but also liberate them from the Roman oppressors. There had already been a number of possible messiahs and Galilee had been the source of several messianic movements.

Little is known of Jesus' childhood but, when he was about 30 years old, he was publicly acclaimed by his cousin, known as John the Baptist. Jesus initially joined with John, who had a substantial following. Then, after John was imprisoned and later executed, Jesus returned to Galilee and began a three-year ministry of teaching and healing. He gathered many followers, in particular 12 male disciples who accompanied him.

Jesus' public preaching was direct, communicated to large groups of ordinary people and often challenged the prevailing teachings of the Jewish religious leaders. He communicated some messages through moral stories, later called **the parables**. Jesus successfully healed people with serious physical and mental illnesses and is believed to have raised at least one person from death. He also performed a number of miracles in response to practical needs such as feeding groups and in response to danger.

Jesus emerges from the accounts in the New Testament as a charismatic figure, but he did not fit the role of messiah in a way convenient to the religious authorities. Firstly he came from Galilee which was regarded as a cultural backwater by the Jews from Judea. Secondly he was openly critical of some of the practices of the religious hierarchy, accused some of the priests of hypocrisy and resolutely refused to take sides on the political issues of Roman occupation.

In the last part of his ministry Jesus prepared his 12 disciples to carry on his teachings, since he anticipated his own death. Jesus went to Jerusalem for the festival of Pesach (see page 15), where he was initially welcomed enthusiastically by the population. However, within a week he had been delivered to the Roman authorities through the actions of the local Jewish religious leaders and one of his disciples, Judas. Jesus was convicted of blasphemy under Jewish law and the Roman governor, Pontius Pilate, was pressured to add the charge of sedition (being a traitor) for which Jesus was then executed by crucifixion, the method used by Romans to kill rebels.

Two days later some of Jesus' disciples found his tomb empty. He appeared to individuals and groups of his followers over a few weeks, emphasising the importance of his teachings and their responsibility to continue. About 40 days after his death, Jesus ascended into heaven, leaving no bodily evidence of his earthly life.

The early Christians were all Jews and some felt that the faith should remain with the Jewish people. However, enough followers disagreed so that the teachings were soon taken to non-Jewish communities and cultures around the Middle East and the Mediterranean. In subsequent centuries Christianity spread further around the world.

Key beliefs

Jesus Christ, from whom the Christian religion takes its name, represents the ideal of a selfless person who championed poor and oppressed people and who died in order to take the sins of humankind upon himself. Christians believe that, although Jesus was born of Mary, his father was God and not Joseph. It is believed that, through his death, Jesus offers salvation to those who recognise the truth.

Christians are monotheistic: worshipping the one God. However, this supreme being is believed to exist in three forms: as God who is perceived as a heavenly **Father**, Jesus who was God's **Son** on earth and as the power of the **Holy Spirit** (or Holy Ghost) that can enter and inspire believers. This threefold nature of God is called the **Trinity**. Disagreement about the exact nature of this concept was one reason for the split between the Western Church and the Orthodox faith. Additionally, some groups, for instance Catholics, place a strong emphasis on the importance of Christ's mother, the Virgin Mary, and different saints. They may pray to God through these saints.

Christians believe that there is only one life and that, after death, believers are united with God in heaven. Some groups are more certain than others that unbelievers will go to hell, a place of torment and suffering. Humans are regarded are essentially sinful and rebellious, but able to be redeemed through penitence and commitment to God.

Some Christian groups promote equality between men and women. Others take the view that women are inferior and possibly a source of sin, a reference to the story of the creation (Genesis in the Old Testament) in which the first woman, Eve, tempted Adam, the first man, to eat from the Tree of Knowledge.

Writings and holy books

THE BIBLE

The Christian holy book is the **Bible**, which is in two parts: the **Old Testament** and the **New Testament**. Some additional writings are known as the **Apocrypha**. The word 'bible' appears to have originated from Byblos, a town in what is now known as the Lebanon which was thriving from about 2500 BCE and was an important market for papyrus, from which early books were made.

Both the Old and New Testaments are subdivided into many sections, written by different people at different historical times and translated into other languages at a later date. The books of the Old Testament are shared with Judaism but are interpreted differently. Christians believe the Old Testament predicts the birth of Christ as Messiah, whereas Jews believe the Messiah is still to come. Jews do not dispute that Jesus was a historical figure, but they disagree with the Christian belief that he was the long-awaited Messiah

The 27 books of the New Testament are specific to Christianity as they recount the life of Christ, his followers and the spread of the Christian faith beyond Palestine. Four Gospels, written by Matthew, Mark, Luke and John, provide slightly different versions of the birth, life and teachings of Jesus Christ. Further sections of the New Testament document the growth of Christian communities around the Middle East and Mediterranean through the letters of apostles and missionaries to the newly established groups. Some Christians, for instance fundamentalist groups and Jehovah's Witnesses, believe the bible to be *literally true* in every word, whereas other Christian groups regard the content as more open to *interpretation*.

The original books of the Old and New Testaments were in a number of languages including Hebrew and Greek. For many centuries Christian services in Europe were conducted in Latin, rather than the local language, and some still are. However, the Bible has been now translated into many of the world's languages.

Christians believe that their lives should be partly guided by the Ten Commandments, given in the Book of Exodus in the Old Testament. However, Jesus in his teachings, for instance on the Sermon on the Mount, explained that a good life was more than following prohibitions without real thought. He described basic rules for living which revolved around reverence for God and a respect for fellow human beings.

STORIES OF THE SAINTS

Other important stories for Christians derive from accounts of lives of the special men and women who have led a life that has been outstanding or have shown great qualities of goodness. Christian saints have been officially recognised (**canonised**) by the Catholic or Orthodox Church, usually long after their death.

Worship

The Christian place of worship is given different names by different groups. The variety of terms include **church** (Protestant or Catholic), **chapel** (Methodist or Baptist), **meeting house** (Quakers) and **Kingdom Hall** (Jehovah's Witnesses). A sign of respect in some Christian places of worship is that men have no head covering and women may be expected to cover their hair with a hat or scarf, but traditions vary. Some Christians show reverence towards the altar and the cross, an especially sacred part of a church, by bowing their head, bending a knee and perhaps also making the sign of the cross against their chest. Some churches also have statues of the Virgin Mary and of important saints, which are treated with great respect. Orthodox churches have distinctive **icons**, which are paintings of the holy family or of saints and are intended as a focus for worship. Prayers are offered to God *through* the icon and not to it.

Sunday is the most significant day for worship but services are held on other days of the week as well. Congregations join in prayers recited together and in silent personal prayer. Some prayers are especially important. For instance, the **Creed** is a statement of shared religious belief and the **Lord's Prayer**, given in the New Testament, is a series of petitions for protection and help to God as the Father. Some Christians believe that prayers that have been said many times over the centuries gain in power.

Worship is also likely to include listening to readings from the Old or New Testament and to a talk from the religious leader, who may be called the **minister**, **priest**, **vicar** or **elder**. Such religious leaders always used to be men, but some Christian groups have accepted women as ordained religious leaders. Some groups, such as the Quakers, have no official religious leader and any member of the congregation can speak up as he or she feels moved.

Some of the most important religious ceremonies are called **sacraments**. Many, but not all Christian groups, hold the service of taking of bread and wine in **Holy Communion**. This event symbolises the last supper which Christ took with his followers before his death and is a reaffirmation of the faith of the congregation.

Strict Christians will neither work nor follow frivolous leisure pursuits on a Sunday, because this is a day of rest. (Christians share the same belief as Jews: that God created the world in six days and then rested on the seventh). The strong influence of the Christian Church in Britain was reflected in secular laws that, until the last decades of the twentieth century, banned a number of activities on Sunday including the opening of most shops.

Christians are likely to pray regularly in a personal way at home. Some homes have a devotional area with holy pictures or a crucifix and some Christians, for instance Catholics, use devotional aides such as a **rosary** (a special set of beads) to support their prayer.

Important symbols

The **cross** is a significant Christian symbol because Christ is believed to have died on the cross (or crucifix) to redeem the sins of humankind. Churches are usually built the shape of a cross and there will normally be a large cross, possibly with a figure of Christ, in a prominent place. Some Christians wear a small version as a necklace or have small crosses as a devotional aide. Some crosses have the figure of Christ to remind Christians of his death but some are empty. This is a reminder that he rose from the dead.

The Christian symbol of the Cross

Rituals and ceremonies

NAMING AND INITIATION

In many Christian groups, there is a service for official acceptance into the religious community. Some groups accept young babies through the ceremony of **christening**. Others postpone this acceptance until adolescence or adulthood, when individuals are judged to be able to make their own personal commitment. This ceremony tends to be called **baptism**. Christening or baptism ceremonies bring the child or adult into contact with holy water, either through a small amount marked into a cross on the forehead or by total immersion. The use of water symbolises the washing away of sin, thought to be a natural state of humans (see page 19).

Groups that christen babies and very young children tend to have a later ceremony called **confirmation** when older children or adolescents make their commitment and can then take Holy Communion (see page 21). Girls usually wear white at this ceremony, as a symbol of purity. Boys wear smart, sober outfits, possibly dark trousers and a white shirt. The Orthodox Church however welcomes babies as full members of the religious community with a combined baptism and confirmation service.

WEDDINGS

Christian weddings are a religious service but have also absorbed cultural traditions over the centuries. Brides usually wear white as a symbol of virginity and carry a bouquet as a symbol of life. The wedding ring is a symbol of eternity and that a couple expect, and are expected, to stay together for life. The throwing of rice or paper confetti symbolises fertility and the hope of children from the union. The top two tiers of the wedding cake are traditionally kept for the christening of the couple's first child.

FUNERALS

The funeral service marks the death of a person, remembrance of their life and confidence in life after death. Mourners traditionally wear black or dark colours and respect is often shown by bringing flowers. Funeral ceremonies vary considerably. Some services are kept very simple, but others may be very elaborate, sometimes followed by a social gathering of the mourners. This is known as a **wake**, in which the deceased person is remembered. The Christian funeral service used always to be one of burial, but cremations are acceptable now for some denominations. The Orthodox Church does not cremate. A commemorative headstone is placed on a grave whereas a plaque may be used as a memorial after cremation. Families may have the cremation urn, with the ashes, interred in part of a cemetry, keep the urn themselves at home or scatter the ashes at a location meaningful to the deceased person.

Festivals

Of the religious celebrations described in this section only **Christmas** has a fixed date. The first day of the **Easter** weekend, **Good Friday**, is always the Friday following the first full moon of the spring equinox, which is one of the two points in the year when day and night are of equal length. Consequently, Easter is a variable date, falling within March or April and the many days of religious significance linked with Easter move accordingly.

- **Lent** lasts from **Ash Wednesday** to **Holy Saturday** of the Easter weekend. The time marks the 40 days that Christ spent in the wilderness, when Christians believe that he resisted the temptations offered by the Devil (the incarnation of all that is evil in the world) and found the strength to start his teachings.
- As mentioned, **Easter** is celebrated in March or April. Although Christmas has become a very significant secular celebration (see also below), Easter is regarded as the more important *religious* festival because the central tenet of Christianity is that Christ died on the cross on Good Friday, yet came back to life on **Easter Sunday**. The **Holy Week** ending in Easter Sunday starts with **Palm Sunday**, a celebration of Christ's entry into Jerusalem riding on a humble donkey, when he was greeted by the local population with palm fronds. (See also page 132.)
- **Ascension Day** is the celebration of Christian belief that, 40 days after his death, Christ disappeared from earthly life, not through death, but through being drawn into heaven with God his Father.
- **Whit Sunday** follows ten days later. Also called **Pentecost**, it is the celebration of how the Holy Spirit came to Christ's remaining disciples, inspiring them to continue his teachings. The power of the spirit enabled them to speak in languages that they had previously not known. The phenomenon of 'speaking in tongues' is significant to Pentecostal Christians who believe that the Holy Spirit can literally enter them and enable speaking in unknown languages.
- **Harvest Festival** is a very ancient celebration of thanks for the year's crops. It was absorbed by Christianity and is celebrated on a Sunday in September or October. Churches often have a display of food, which traditionally is distributed to the less well-off people of the parish. (See also page 134.)
- **Christmas Day** is celebrated on the 25th December by the Western Church and 6th January by the Eastern Orthodox Church. The festival

marks the birth of Jesus Christ, believed to be the Son of God, although he was born to a human mother, Mary. **Advent** is the four weeks that lead up to Christmas. Christians may attend Midnight Mass on Christmas Eve and this service is a special Holy Communion. (See also page 129.)

Application to daily living

Food and drink

There are no consistent rules about diet that apply across Christianity. Some Christians quote sections of the Bible to support an anti-vegetarian stance: that God provided the creatures for the express use of humankind, including their nutritional needs. Some Christians avoid alcohol, for example Mormons and some Baptists and Methodists. (Christian groups that avoid alcohol and hold the service of Holy Communion, celebrate with non-alcoholic wine or other drinks.)

Periods of fasting or giving up particular foods used to be common practice within the Christian faith but is much less usual now. Some Christians still avoid meat on Fridays because of the link to Good Friday, when Christ died on the cross. Some give up one or two foods for Lent to remember the testing of Christ in the wilderness. The type of food given up for Lent is now usually a treat, like sugar in coffee or eating chocolate. Catholics may fast on Ash Wednesday, the first day of Lent. Christians from the Orthodox Church are more likely to continue to follow the religious tradition of avoiding meat, eggs and milk products for all of Lent.

Pilgrimages

Special journeys to show religious commitment and to strengthen religious faith used to be more common in Christianity. For instance, from the sixth century many pilgrims used to travel to Canterbury cathedral to see the holy relics (items of religious significance, often clothing, possessions or body parts of a holy person). The ancient path along the Surrey Downs is still known as the Pilgrims' Way. Christian pilgrimage still occurs, for instance:

- Catholics make the journey to Rome to be part of the large audiences addressed by the Pope, the spiritual leader of the Catholic Christian community.
- Some Christians make a pilgrimage to Lourdes in France in order to seek relief from their own pain or illness, or that of a friend or relative.
- There is some evidence that the onset of the millennium in the year 2000 has spurred a revival of interest in pilgrimage, with large gatherings

expected at what were important sacred sites in previous centuries. One example is Santiago De Compostela in northern Spain, where it is believed the remains of James, one of Christ's disciples, are buried.

Islam

As an important gesture of reverence and respect, a specific Arabic writing symbol is used each time the name of the **Prophet Muhammad** is mentioned. It is composed of the words 'Salla-llahu alaihi wa sallam' and the letters S.A.W. are used in English translations. In full, the words mean 'peace and blessings of Allah upon him'. Specific phrases are also used after the names of other Prophets and significant historical religious figures, for instance, the Prophet Isa (peace be upon him).

Background

Islam developed as a world faith about 1400 years ago. The Prophet Muhammad S.A.W. was a respected and prosperous merchant in Makkah (Mecca) who reached a point of personal crisis when he was 40 years old. He sought the loneliness of the desert to find some answers. During that experience, the Prophet Muhammad S.A.W. had visions that he had been called upon by the angel Jibrai'il (Gabriel) to be the prophet of the one God, **Allah**. The Prophet Muhammad S.A.W. continued to receive revelations from Jibrai'il over a period of 23 years and these insights were recited to his companions. The revelations were initially committed to memory and recited as an oral tradition but were later written down.

After the first revelations the Prophet Muhammad S.A.W. returned to his home town of Makkah to preach, but opposition grew to his teachings and he left for Madinah (Medina) in 622 CE. This year was the **hijrah** (journey or emigration), of the Prophet Muhammad S.A.W. and marks the beginning of the Islamic calendar and years are counted from this event.

The Prophet Muhammad S.A.W. continued to receive revelations from Allah, that he was merciful and all-powerful, controlling the course of events in the world. All these revelations were gathered into the **Qur'an** (from the Arabic word meaning to recite, because most of this sacred book is in the form of the words of Allah that the Prophet Muhammad S.A.W. was commanded to proclaim to the world). There are 114 divisions of the Qur'an, called **surahs**.

The term **Islam** comes from the Arabic word aslama, which means to submit, so Islam means the peace attained through a willing obedience to Allah's divine guidance. Followers of the faith are known as Muslims, which means people who have accepted Islam by making the key declaration of faith, the **Shahadah** (see page 28).

Key beliefs

Muslims believe that the Prophet Muhammad S.A.W. was the final Prophet in the chain of revelation and communication between Allah and humankind. Ibrahim (Abraham), Musa (Moses) and other important figures from Jewish early history and the Old Testament, and Isa (Jesus Christ), were earlier prophets whom Muslims believe should be respected. Muslims do not believe that Isa was the Son of God, but he was a significant prophet born of the virgin Maryam (Mary).

Muslims believe that the world is based on justice tempered with mercy. They believe there is one life only and that Allah will judge people according to their behaviour and assign them to paradise or hell on the day of judgement. **Akhirah** is the concept of life after earthly death. It is believed that angels record the details of everyone's life and that each individual has two angels who watch over him or her. Muslims believe that everyone has an allotted span of life but that only Allah knows how long this is for each individual. It is therefore the duty of Muslims to approach each day as if it were their last and to be ready for Allah's call when that comes.

Islam teaches that all people are equal regardless of age and race. Men and women are believed to be equal, although their responsibilities are not the same, and they have equal rights of education and property. The interpretation of the principle of equal but different for the sexes varies considerably in different Muslim societies around the world today and in some countries women are not afforded anything like equal rights with men.

There are four key aspects to a proper Muslim life:

1. **Tawhid**: this is the belief in the absolute Oneness of Allah. It is completely unacceptable to envisage anything that could be equal to or a partner with Allah. **Shirk** (meaning association) is the concept of this forbidden area of belief. Muslims believe that the attributes of Allah are revealed within the Qur'an, that there are signs of Allah's creation throughout nature and that humans are the best of that creation.
2. **Iman**: this means faith and covers the details of Muslim beliefs. The

Qur'an is very important but other writings are believed to be a significant source of guidance. These include the Scrolls of Ibrahim, the **Tawrah** (the Jewish Torah), **Zabur** (the Book of Psalms) and **Injil** (Gospel). Iman also encompasses key beliefs that were summarised on page 27.

3. **Ibadah**: this means worship and belief in action. Muslims are expected to follow the requirements of the five pillars of the faith (see page 29) and to worship in the appropriate way. Muslims are also required to implement the rules of life laid down in the Shari'ah (see below) and to deal with this application even in a non-Muslim environment. It is important that Muslims remain aware of their obligation of **Da'wah**, which is to alert non-Muslims to Islam, either through the good example of their own daily life or specific preaching.

4. **Akhlaq**: focuses on proper character, moral conduct and ethical attitudes. Muslims show appropriate behaviour through respectful actions towards family and other people. Important qualities include patience, honesty, taking appropriate responsibility and charitable actions towards people who are poor or needy.

Writings and holy books

The **Qur'an** is the sacred book of Islam, and contains the revelations that The Prophet Muhammad S.A.W. received from Allah. The Qur'an was revealed in Arabic so this is the language of Islamic worship, holy writings and law whatever the daily language or languages spoken by believers. Although the Qur'an was written down after the Prophet's death, committing the holy book to memory is still very important for Muslims and is part of what children are taught in their Qur'an classes.

The **Shari'ah** forms the details of Islamic law. It is based on the Qur'an and other writings describing the example set by the Prophet Muhammad S.A.W. Interpretations of the Shari'ah vary and some Muslim communities are considerably stricter than others. The term **sunna** refers to the practice of the Prophet as held within traditions of what is permitted or not.

Worship and religious practice

Individual Muslims are expected to create a direct link with Allah through the five essential Islamic practices, known as the **Pillars of the Faith**.

- The First Pillar is **Shahadah**, to repeat the key Islamic belief which is the statement that 'There is no god except Allah, the Prophet Muhammad S.A.W. is the Messenger of Allah'.

- The Second Pillar is **Salah**, prayer in the manner prescribed by the Prophet Muhammad S.A.W. five times in every day at dawn, midday, afternoon, sunset and night. Before prayer, individuals cleanse their face, head, arms, feet and ankles. Prayer can be undertaken at home or elsewhere. At all times of prayer Muslims turn towards Makkah and they follow a series of movements that unite the whole congregation in worship as they follow the lead of the Imam in reciting words of prayer from the Qur'an. The Friday midday prayer is the special time that Muslims congregate at the Mosque for **Jumu'ah** (or Salat-ul-Jumu'ah) when there is also a talk, **Khutbah**. Friday is not a day off from ordinary life for Muslims. Shops and businesses close only for the hour or so needed to attend Jumu'ah.
- The Third Pillar is **Zakah**, a moral obligation to share one's wealth by giving to less fortunate people in the community.
- The Fourth Pillar is **Sawm**, fasting in the prescribed way during Ramadan (see page 32). The intention of fasting is one of internal thanksgiving, of discipline and a patient waiting upon Allah who guides and provides. The Prophet Muhammad S.A.W. said that, of all the duties of worship, Sawm was most loved by Allah since only He could observe it.
- The Fifth Pillar is **Hajj**, a pilgrimage to the sacred mosques at Makkah which is expected once in a lifetime from all followers of Islam who have the health and financial ability to do so. Many pilgrims make the journey in the last month of the Muslim year. A male Muslim who has completed Hajj is called Hajji and a female called Hajjah. Muslims can visit Makkah at any time of the year as a form of worship in action called **Umrah**, but this visit is not a substitute for Hajj.

For some services, Muslim men attend the Mosque alone and women often pray at home. Women and children do attend the Mosque and there are separate sections for the two sexes. Mosques, even smaller ones, will usually have a dome and minaret. In Muslim societies, people are reminded to pray five times a day by calls which are broadcast from the minaret. Decorations in a mosque are intricate geometric patterns and stylised flowers, but they never show people or animals, since this is believed to be against the wish of Allah.

Symbols

The star and crescent moon are important symbols in Islam. One reason is that in hot countries people travel in the cool of the night and the stars and moon guide them. These heavenly bodies guide and give light in the same way that Islam guides the faithful.

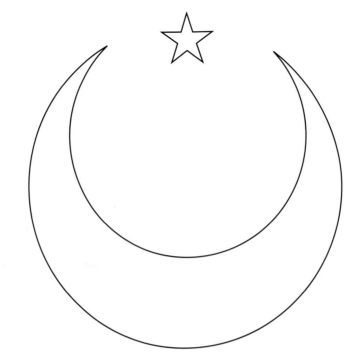

The Star and Crescent Moon of Islam

Rituals and ceremonies

NAMING AND INITIATION

The birth of a baby is regarded as a blessing (**barakah**) and newborns are greeted with the taste of something sweet, like honey, on their tongue. The father will hold the baby close and whisper a prayer into each ear. The baby's head is shaved for the special naming ceremony and money is given to charity, by tradition silver of the same weight as the baby's hair but in practice often more.

Children are believed to be able to distinguish between right and wrong by seven years of age and so religious education starts then. Children will attend Qur'an classes in the Mosque or with a teacher close to their home. At this point children learn to read and write Arabic, if the language is not used in the family.

WEDDINGS

A wedding contract is signed by both the bride and groom but not necessarily at the same time as the marriage ceremony. The occasion of signing the contract is called **nikka**. The contract is a human, rather than religious agreement, but the couple are also assumed to be committing themselves to live according the teachings of the Qur'an.

Asian brides, of different faiths, often get married in red or a deep pink-coloured silk, embroidered with gold thread. Complex **mehndi** patterns may be painted on the bride's hands and feet and these give a warm red colour, red being a colour of celebration. Men wear either traditional dress from their cultural background or a western style suit.

FUNERALS

Muslims bury their dead and the body of the deceased is placed to face Makkah. Funeral services tend to be simple, in order to show that all Muslims are equal in death. Ideally, members of the immediate family do not cook for themselves for 40 days and food is brought by relatives and neighbours.

Celebrations

Muslim religious festivals are determined by lunar sightings rather than specific dates within the lunar calendar. So, in comparison with the Western calendar, the festivals move earlier each year and the exact date cannot usually be given in advance, although it is known within a day or so. The night sky is often obscured by cloud over Europe, so Muslims in Britain are guided in the timings of important festivals by lunar sightings in their country of origin or from Makkah.

The festivals within Islam all have specific religious meaning and, although some are a time of celebration for families and friends, the events tend not to have the layers of cultural or secular tradition that have become associated with some festivals from other world faiths. The main events include:

- **Hijrah** (the journey of the Prophet Muhammad S.A.W. from Makkah to Madinah) is celebrated at the beginning of each Muslim year. The time celebrates the establishing of the Muslim community and gifts may be exchanged. (See also page 137.)
- **Milad-un-Nabi** falls within the third month of the Muslim calendar and is a time when the birth of the Prophet Muhammad S.A.W. is remembered (571 CE) and the story of his life recounted in detail. Some Muslims celebrate at this time, offering food to friends and neighbours, although the celebrations are muted since they are also remembering the death of the Prophet Muhammad S.A.W., believed to have happened in this same month.

- **Mi'raj-Un-Nabi** celebrates the time when Prophet Muhammad S.A.W. ascended into heaven. The time is marked by prayer, reading from the Qur'an and gifts to the poor.
- **Laylat-Ul-Bara'at** is a time when Allah assesses the behaviour of Muslims and so is an opportunity for reflection and penitence in preparation for Ramadan.
- **Ramadan**, the ninth month of the Muslim year starts with the first sighting of the crescent-shaped new moon. This time is important because it was the month in which the Qur'an was first revealed to the Prophet Muhammad S.A.W. This event is recalled on **Laylat-ul-Qadr**, the Night of Power, which is the eve of the twenty-sixth day of fast during Ramadan. During Ramadan the Qur'an is read in its entirety in the Mosque during the hours of prayer, in 90-minute periods of time. Muslims are required to abstain from food and drink from dawn until sunset for the six weeks of Ramadan, until the next new moon is sighted. With the requirements of fasting, the pace of life within a Muslim community slows down and Ramadan is a time for reflection on spiritual standards. Muslims are also expected to refrain from bad habits such as lying or anger so it can be a time when relationships are reaffirmed and reconciliation is encouraged.
- **Id-ul-Fitr** marks the end of Ramadan and is a celebration ending the long period of daylight fast. The festival lasts between two to five days and is celebrated by a special meal, the wearing of new or best clothes, an exchange of cards and presents for children. (See also page 138.)
- **Id-ul-Adha** marks the willingness of the Prophet Ibrahim (Abraham of the Jewish Torah and Christian Old Testament) to sacrifice his son Isma'il (Ishmael) to Allah, and Isma'il's willingness to make the personal sacrifice of his life. The story as told in the three world faiths is that God (however envisaged by each faith) caused a ram to appear to be sacrificed instead. This four-day festival, within the final month of the Muslim calendar, coincides with the end of the annual pilgrimage to Makkah (the Hajj). Families celebrate together and eat a special meal, of lamb or sheep. As at Id-ul-Fitr, the festival is a time to give to those less fortunate in the community. (See also page 139.)

Application to daily living

DIET

Muslim families are required to avoid pork in any form and also alcohol. Any meat or poultry must be **Halal** which means lawful, whereas **Haram** means unlawful. Acceptable meat and poultry is produced by the method of slaughter that allows a body to bleed (the same method used by Kosher butchers for Jewish people). The meat or poultry is dedicated to Allah by the Imam.

STYLE OF DRESS

Muslim women are expected to wear **hijab**, which means modest dress covering all the body except the face and hands. Muslim communities and families vary in the strictness of application of hijab and the exact style will depend on the cultural traditions of the local Muslim community. Likewise men may wear loose trousers and tunic and a small head covering for the crown of the head, or they may wear local dress except for religious occasions.

Further resources

You will find suggestions for reading further about Judaism, Christianity and Islam at the end of Chapter 3 on pages 56–58.

Children with varied family backgrounds come together in nursery

3

World Faiths II: Hinduism, Buddhism and Sikhism

Introduction

These three world faiths have been placed together because Hinduism is the root of both Buddhism and Sikhism. The latter two faiths developed, in their very different ways, as reactions against some beliefs within Hinduism. Each faith has different sub-groups and, as you read both this chapter and the previous one, it is very important to remember that there is variety in all the main world faiths.

Hinduism

Background

This religious tradition appears to have become established about 5000 years ago. The name 'Hinduism' is far more recent and dates from about 800 years ago, when Muslims invading India wanted to distinguish the existing religion from Islam. 'Hindu' was the Persian word for Indian and has been retained to describe this large religious and cultural group. Although Hinduism is the generally accepted term in the West, followers of the faith often refer to themselves as **Sanatan Dharma**, referring to the eternal or imperishable religion.

Key beliefs

Hindus believe in **Brahman**, the ultimate source of being, an all-pervading reality from which everything emerges, in which it rests and into which all life is ultimately dissolved. Brahman is itself impersonal and formless, but can be understood and worshipped through deities or gods that personify its many aspects. In one sense, Hinduism can be seen as a monotheistic religion, since all deities are ultimately Brahman. However, the different aspects of Brahman are revered in such detail and through separate entities that for all intents Hinduism operates as a polytheistic faith (worshipping many gods).

Three important deities, known as **Trimuti**, represent and control the key functions for life: **Brahma** (the power of creation), **Vishnu** (the sustainer of life) and **Shiva** (destroyer of what is old to make way for new life). They also personify and control the three **gunas** (meaning a rope or quality) of goodness, passion and ignorance which permeate all living matter.

Deities sometimes descend in human form and this is the concept of **avatar.** The most common example is that of Vishnu who is believed to have appeared in human form ten times, the best known being **Krishna** (who is regarded as almost having the status of a deity) and **Rama**. Hindus believe that the **Buddha** (see Buddhism, page 41) was the ninth time that Vishnu took human form.

Many other aspects of the ultimate reality are manifested through **devas** (meaning someone or something that has godlike qualities). Each deva possesses specific individual powers and may appear in human or animal form. For example, **Lakshmi,** the wife of Vishnu, represents wealth and prosperity. **Ganesh** is the deva who is able to remove obstacles in the lives of those who worship him. The variety of Hindu festivals usually feature different individual devas and Hindus can worship the deva or devas of their choice.

Hindus believe in reincarnation: that souls are reborn in an everlasting cycle from birth to death and then to rebirth. The quality of one's current life is directly affected by behaviour in previous lives. The concept of **karma** (meaning action) refers to this relationship of cause and effect. The term **samsara** describes the world, the place in which **transmigration** occurs, which is the soul's passage through a series of lives as different people or species. **Nirvana** is a peaceful state of the cessation of all material existence and is achieved by very few individuals.

The way to salvation in Hinduism is through the three **marg** (paths): **karma-yoga** (dedicating the fruits of one's work to God), **jnana-yoga** (the path of knowledge) and **bhakti-yoga** (loving devotion to God). **Raja Yoga** is also sometimes included (self control and meditation). **Yoga** means a form of communion, a union of the soul with the ultimate being and is a process of discipline that promotes that relationship. (The word is used widely in the West just to refer to the physical and mental discipline of yoga exercises.)

There are four aims in life.

1. **Dharma** is often translated as religious duty but means more literally that which sustains one's existence.

2. **Artha** refers to the duty of a householder to acquire wealth and property.
3. **Kama** means a regulated sense of enjoyment.
4. Finally, **Moksha** is the ultimate liberation from the continuous cycle of birth and death.

Important Hindu texts

There are two main groups of important Hindu scriptures.

1. **Shruti**, or revealed scripture, includes the **Vedas** and the **Upanishads**.
2. **Smirti**, or remembered scriptures, include the **Bhagavad Gita** and the **Puranas** (meaning ancient). The **Bhagavata Purana** tells of the birth, childhood and early life of Krishna who, as a significant manifestation of Vishnu, is revered in his own right.

The four **Vedas** (meaning knowledge) are written in the ancient language of **Sanskrit**, now spoken only by scholars. The **Upanishads** (meaning to sit down near) explain the teachings of the Vedas and are sacred texts based on the teaching of a guru to a disciple. Key beliefs in Hinduism are also communicated through epic stories, two important examples being the **Ramayana** (meaning Rama's travels) and the **Mahabharata**.

The Ramayana is about 4000 years old and tells the story of Rama's physical voyage from one end of the Indian sub-continent to another in his perilous quest to save his wife Sita. Gods and demons both help and hinder Rama in his quest, which is a test of his faith and courage. The epic tale (24,000 couplets in length) is also symbolic of Rama's spiritual journey. The story illustrates the working of dharma, of honour and duty; Rama's devotion to Sita and to his people, are in a higher sense the expression of a love that demanded the sacrifice of Rama's own personal freedom and wishes.

The Mahabharata (90,000 couplets long) recounts the feud between cousins from the Pandava and Kaurava families which had vast national repercussions. The tale also communicates an ethical and spiritual narrative about morality and devotion. The **Bhagavad Gita** (The Song of the Lord) spoken by Krishna, and a very significant scripture for most Hindus, is a part of this epic and is also considered to be an Upanishad.

Both these epic tales reflect the Hindu belief that history is divided into cycles. At the beginning of each cycle, there is order but throughout four **yugas** (ages) standards deteriorate until the gods intervene to destroy and remake the world. The present, fourth age is **kali yuga**, an age of quarrelling and hypocrisy.

Worship

Hindus worship at the **Mandir** where different statues of devas are believed to represent a particular attribute of the divine presence. The mandir is viewed like the palace of a king and worship resembles the level of respect and hospitality that would be offered to a royal personage. Consequently, worship may involve the offering of food and beautiful flowers to the statue of a deva and the ritual washing of the statue. The term **puja** refers to the variety of forms of worship in the home or the Mandir.

During the ceremony in the mandir a priest may read from the Vedas, but Hindus from the first three **castes** (see page 40) can also read prayers or lead a **mantra** (a short sacred text that is repeated to focus the mind). Worshippers make gifts of money or flowers to one of the shrines within the Mandir. There may be devotional hymns or songs (**bhajan**). The **arti** ceremony is a welcoming event in which articles like incense or lamps are offered to the deity or to saintly people who are present. **Pravachan** is a sermon given to the congregation. Hindu communities welcome visits from holy people who have travelled from India. Worship occurs, especially on Sundays, but also on other days of the week.

Worship at home is regarded as equally important as attendance at the Mandir. Many homes have a household shrine with a statue or picture of the preferred deva. Some homes may have a room set aside for worship. There may be a **mandala**, which is a complex geometric picture that represents the universe. Hindus from the first three castes worship three times a day and men wear the **janeu (**sacred thread, see below).

Rituals

NAMING AND INITIATION

Samskar (or samskara) is the term for a sacrament that initiates a new stage of life. There are 16 samskars in total, although many Hindu groups do not practise all of them. Three samskars are celebrated while the mother of an unborn child is still pregnant. The newborn baby is washed and the holy symbol of **aum** (see page 39) is marked on his or her tongue with a golden pen using honey (the fourth samskar). At 12 days old the baby is named in a ceremony, which is the fifth samskar. Then, at one year old the baby's head is shaved as a symbol of losing any sin left from past lives (the sixth samskar).

Boys of the first three castes become part of the Hindu community at the age of eight to ten years through the rite of **Upanayana**, the ceremony of being invested with the sacred thread. The priest will pray in front of the sacred fire, a symbol of energy and purity. He blesses the thread and ties it loosely with a special knot to hang from the boy's shoulder across to his waist. The ceremony shows that the boys are starting a new and pure life. The rite used to be a sign that boys would now begin study under a guru or holy teacher. However, in many Hindu communities boys start less intensive religious study, or minimally learn a special prayer, the **Gayatri Mantra**.

WEDDINGS

Marriage is seen as a religious duty for a man and arranged marriages are common. The event is viewed as very important because it brings together two families, not just the man and woman involved. Families often involve sons and daughters in the choice of partner (see the comment on page 15). Both bride and groom are usually dressed in bright colours and elaborately decorated clothes. The bride has an array of jewellery and her hands and feet are painted in complex geometric patterns with henna.

The couple make their promises before the supreme being, believed to be present in the sacred fire. Following the custom of **satapandi** (seven steps) they walk four times round the sacred fire. The seven steps symbolise seven duties to each other. After the final step, the bride and groom place their right hands against their partner's heart. There are no written signatures, since it is believed that the commitment has been made by the couple's feet and written invisibly on their hearts.

The ceremony of **havan** is the basis of many Hindu rituals and ceremonies such as marriage. During havan, offerings of ghee (clarified butter) and grains are made into fire within the **havan kund**, a special square or pyramid-shaped container.

FUNERALS

Hindu funerals are cremations and the fire is set by the deceased's eldest son. The ashes are gathered three days later and ideally are thrown with sacred marigold flowers onto the waters of the Ganges, a holy river. Hindus living in countries other than India may arrange for the ashes to be sent for scattering on the holy waters. For ten days after the funeral the family makes offerings of rice balls and milk at a shrine.

Symbols

The significant Hindu symbol is the written form of aum, written sometimes as om. The symbol and sound is sacred because it represents a sense of the ultimate. It is the sound used at the beginning and the end of prayers.

The Aum Symbol

The **lotus flower** is another Hindu symbol, standing for purity, fertility, good fortune and progress.

Festivals and celebrations

- **Holi** is a spring festival of colours associated with Krishna and an event which crosses the boundaries of caste. It happens in February or March and is a lively event. Different legends are associated with Holi including the miraculous saving of Prahlada through his faith in Vishnu and Rama and how the baby Krishna defeated the female demon Putana. (See also page 140.)
- **Raksha Bandhan** takes place in July or August and celebrates a promise made by brothers to sisters, or by males to a close female friend, that they will protect their sister or friend. The girls make or buy twisted red and gold thread bracelets (**rakhi**) which they give to the boys. The focus of the festival is to recognise and strengthen the bond between brothers and sisters. (See also page 141.)
- **Ganesh Charturhti** is a ten-day festival in September focused on the deva Ganesh who has the power to remove obstacles from the lives of worshippers. Clay images of Ganesh are set within shrines and immersed in water at the end of the festival.

- **Dassehra** lasts ten days in September or October. For some Hindus this festival celebrates the victory of Rama. Others celebrate the nine nights of **Navaratri** preceding Dassehra, and focus on the deva Durga (who is also known or takes the form of Kali or Parvati, wife of Shiva). Durga is a symbol of motherhood but for some Hindus also has a warlike form.
- **Divali** is a five-day festival in October or November. One important theme is reverence for the deva Lakshmi, the wife of Vishnu, who is associated with wealth and good fortune and who is said to visit every Hindu home once a year. According to one Hindu calendar this is now the start of a new year. The second important theme is the account of Rama's rescue of his wife Sita from the demon king Ravana and his return to his birthplace of Ayodhya after 14 years in exile. (See also page 142).

Application to daily living

THE CASTE SYSTEM

Varna (meaning colour) refers to the traditional four main divisions of Hindu society. The classification appears originally to have been determined by the talents shown by individuals. **Jati** (caste) was an occupational kinship system that developed into a rigid way of life so that individuals' place in society was determined utterly by the family into which they were born. A fifth group, the so-called **untouchables**, were outside the caste system completely and undertook work that nobody else would do.

Two major faiths that emerged from Hinduism, Buddhism (see page 41) and Sikhism (see page 48), specifically rejected the caste system. Twentieth-century development in India has included some attempt to return to a more flexible determination of individuals' social position.

PILGRIMAGE

Hinduism stresses the importance of **yatra** (pilgrimage) to sacred sites of religious significance. For example:

- The city of Varanisi (Benares) is sacred to Shiva and one of the holiest pilgrimage sites, also because it is located by the river Ganga (Ganges), the most sacred of all the holy rivers.
- Gangotri is important as the source of the Ganga.
- Vrindavan is a sacred village linked with Krishna's youth.
- Ayodhya is important as the birthplace of Rama.

Pilgrimages may be made for different reasons: in the fulfilment of a promise, to respond to the birth of a child, in the spirit of atonement or humility or to discover one's heritage.

Dress

The dress style of Hindus is influenced by the Indian cultural origins of many families. Women may wear **saris** and men full trousers and a long tunic known as **pyjama** and **kameez**. Some men may wear a **dhoti**, a wraparound length of cloth instead of trousers. Young Hindu people living in Europe often wear Western-style clothes except for special occasions.

Diet

In Hinduism the cow is a sacred animal because it symbolises the earth and the bounty made available to humankind. Hindus use the products of the living cow, like milk, but will never kill the animal and so avoid beef meat in any form. Some Hindus are vegetarian, feeling that the sacred nature of the cow should be extended to all living creatures.

Hygiene

Some Hindus follow a specific approach to hygiene: the right hand is used consistently for eating and the left for personal hygiene including toileting.

Buddhism

• *A note on terms* •

I have continued to be guided by the SCAA glossary of terms, as described on page 10. In the West, Buddhist terms derived from both Pali and Sanskrit are common. The glossary suggests the Pali version, unless the Sanskrit is the more usual.

Background

Buddhism originated some 2500 years ago in India. **Siddattha Gotama**, (sometimes given as Siddharta Gautama), the founder of Buddhism was a prince who was born around 560 BCE. Gotama's father was a rajah and he was raised in wealth and comfort. It had been prophesied to his father that his son would either be a great ruler or a homeless wanderer and, to ensure the former, Gotama's father sheltered his son from knowledge of the outside world.

Despite his life of luxury, by adulthood Gotama felt dissatisfied and made three journeys beyond the limits of the palace where he was shocked by the suffering of ordinary people. On a fourth journey he met a monk who travelled dependent on the charity of others and Gotama decided to follow this course. With a small group of followers he dedicated himself for six or seven years to a traditional Hindu pattern of self-denial, but this experience did not answer his deeper questions and he turned to meditation. During the month of Wesak (May) when the moon was full, Gotama spent three nights in deep contemplation. He gained insight into universal truths and emerged as the **Buddha**, meaning the awakened or enlightened one. The fig tree under which the Buddha had sat became known as the Bodhi Tree (the Tree of Wisdom).

As an enlightened one, the Buddha could have entered nirvana, a state of secure and perfect peace beyond the cycles of death and rebirth. He chose to stay and share his insights as a teacher. He gave his first inspirational sermon, known as The Turning of the Wheel of Law, in which he explained the basis for a way of life that has become Buddhism (see Key beliefs below). The Buddha rejected the existing Hindu caste system and drew followers from different walks of life. He was initially resistant to the involvement of women, on the grounds that they kept the cycle of rebirth in motion. However, his stepmother and cousin persuaded him to admit women.

Buddhism spread beyond India to influence societies throughout the East. **Theravada** Buddhism (the way of the elders) is the oldest form of the faith and was established in Sri Lanka and the South East Asia. **Mahayana** (the Great Way or Vehicle) Buddhism developed an emphasis on **Bodhisattvas**, ideal people who, like the Buddha, postpone nirvana in order to teach and help others. Buddhists in this tradition believe that there will continue to be such wise teachers. One of the most important is **Avalokiteswara**, the embodiment of compassion, who is believed to be reincarnated in each **Dalai Lama** (meaning teacher) of Tibet. **Zen Buddhism** developed in the Far East, where it blended with Shintoism (an animist religion) in Japan and with Taoism (a philosophical system as ancient as Buddhism) in China.

Key beliefs

Buddhism differs from the other five major world faiths (described in this chapter and Chapter 2) in that Buddhists do not share specific religious beliefs about a deity and what such an entity requires of followers. Buddhism is a way of wisdom in which understanding is more important than particular beliefs.

The Buddha himself was definitely neither a god nor a messenger of any god or gods. The ethical and spiritual system established through **Dhamma** (the Buddha's teachings or ultimate truth) is one of self-redemption, that humans have the ability and responsibility to lead a good life. The aim of Buddhists is to strive to follow the example set by the Buddha in his life and to guide their own life by his teachings.

The Buddha explained the fundamental insights that had been revealed during his nights of meditation. His teachings were based on **Four Noble Truths**, which were that:

1. All life is Suffering (**dukkha**).
2. There is a Cause (**samudaya**) of Suffering.
3. There is a Cessation of Suffering (**nirodha**)
4. There is a path (**magga**) that leads to the Cessation of Suffering (the state of nirvana).

The term **dukkha** describes the nature of existence as perceived by the Buddha. The word is usually translated as 'suffering' but has a broader meaning that also encompasses imperfection and an unsatisfactory or ill state. The suffering or pain may be physical or emotional or a general sense of dissatisfaction. The Buddha explained that dukkha was caused by **tanha**, which means a craving arising from ignorance. Suffering is caused by people's desires that lead to greed and selfishness. They crave for the wrong things in life, or for the right things but in a wrong way. Suffering could be prevented by following a right way of life.

The Buddha also identified that life is characterised by change. The term **anicca** described the instability of all things, that life is transient and impermanent and that includes the self. The term **anatta** describes the insubstantial state of human life, that there is no permanent state of self and that people change all the time. The Buddha also believed that there was no soul. The Buddha explained that human beings make the mistake of putting a misplaced value on things or people. Yet nothing in the material world is worthy of reverence, nothing can be depended upon and all is ultimately unstable.

The final goal of all human endeavour, that of the cessation of suffering, is reached by following the Middle Path: one of neither self-indulgence nor extreme self-denial. The Way is known as the **Noble Eightfold Path** and should be followed for a proper life, whether or not people reach the final goal. The Noble Eightfold Path consists of the following steps.

1. **Right View** (Knowledge or Understanding): that life should be valued for itself and that followers should recognise the Four Noble Truths.
2. **Right Thought** (or Attitude): an outlook of goodwill to other people and peaceableness, attitudes far removed from malice, hate or cruelty.
3. **Right Speech**: speech should be wise, truthful and directed towards reconciliation rather than making matters worse. Buddhists should avoid lies or idle gossip.

4. **Right Action**: care should be taken over behaviour so that actions are moral. Murder, stealing and adultery are especially prohibited.
5. **Right Livelihood** (or Occupation): Buddhists should ensure that the way they earn their living cannot harm others.
6. **Right Effort**: attention must be given to fostering noble thoughts, words and actions and preventing evil impulses.
7. **Right Mindfulness**: is a level of self-awareness and careful consideration so that desires do not drive thoughts, words or actions.
8. **Right Concentration** (or Composure): is achieved through the discipline of meditation, calm thoughts removed from everyday concerns, in which Buddhists focus on their search for truth and knowledge.

The combination of wisdom (paths 1 and 2), ethical conduct (paths 3, 4 and 5) and mental discipline (paths 6, 7 and 8) required by the Noble Eightfold Path rest upon qualities such as valuing life, being considerate to others, avoiding harmful behaviour and focusing the mind through meditation.

Although the Buddha rejected some Hindu beliefs, he continued to believe in reincarnation, kamma (karma) and the possibility of nirvana. However, the Buddha envisaged that humans were able to influence their progress towards nirvana through following the Noble Eightfold Path. Through a right way of living it is possible to generate positive kamma, the good effects of which can be experienced by oneself and by those around a person. The Buddha also envisaged nirvana not as the annihilation of self, but as a transformed state of human consciousness, which can be glimpsed through the discipline of meditation. A key part of the Buddha's teaching was that humans were naturally pure of heart but that this state was obscured by greed, hatred and ignorance. A life that strives to be free of evil and actively good will reveal the pureness once more.

Important Buddhist texts

The teachings of the Buddha were initially passed on by word of mouth and only later committed to a written form. The ancient Asian language of **Pali** is used in the holy texts of the Theravada school while Sanskrit is used for the general Mahayana (The Great Way or Vehicle, the teachings of Buddhism).

The **Lotus Sutra** is an important scripture in the Mahayana tradition. it describes the virtues of Bodhisattvas and their contribution towards the enlightenment of those who attend to their teachings. The Lotus Sutra emphasises that all beings have the potential of a Buddha-nature and can attain enlightenment. The **Dhammapada** is a famous scripture comprising 423 verses. The **Metta Sutta** describes the nature of loving kindness. (Sutta means text, which is also the word of the Buddha.)

There are three collections of holy scriptures. The **Vinaya Pitaka** covers the special disciplines for ordained monks and nuns and also includes some stories and teachings. The **Sutta Pitaka** is mainly key teachings that form the basic scripture for all Buddhists. The **Abhidhamma Pitaka** is a systematic and more advanced scripture covering the teachings of the Sutta Pitaka at a level appropriate for advanced study, such as the nature of nirvana, and the more complicated meditation techniques. Pitaka means basket and the **Tipitaka** are the three baskets. The idea is a way to describe how the three different collections of Buddhist scriptures apply and are more appropriate to three different groups: the general population, to ordained monks or nuns and to advanced students.

The teachings within Buddhism are communicated through important stories including the **Jakata** (birth story) which recounts the previous lives of the Buddha and other stories about his life as Siddattha Gotama. A range of stories illustrate the **Brahma Viharas** which are the four sublime states of loving kindness, compassion, sympathetic joy and evenness of mind.

Worship

Buddhists come together to worship in the **Vihara**. They venerate the **Three Treasures**: the Buddha as teacher and embodiment of the potential in everyone, the Dhamma (the Buddha's teachings) and the **Sangha** (the Buddhist community). Images and statues of the Buddha in the Vihara or shrines are to remind Buddhists of the Dhamma and to focus the mind. Buddhists do not pray to Buddha (who is definitely not regarded as a god). Praying in this way would be a pointless exercise since the Buddha is believed to have passed into nirvana. A Vihara may also have statues of important Bodhisattvas. A Buddhist home will also have a shrine where family members can meditate in calmness on a daily basis.

Meditation is very important for Buddhists because it is through this process that one can attain an inner calm and mental clarity. Some Buddhists use **mantras** (a key saying repeated over and over again) or **mandalas** (complex patterns) in order to focus during meditation and remove distractions.

Buddhism has ordained monks, nuns and priests but the faith stresses the ability of *ordinary* Buddhists to guide their own lives by the Noble Eightfold

Path. The Vinaya Pitaka, the life rules for monks and nuns, are stricter than those for the general population and include requirements such as celibacy. Monks and nuns are permitted only limited possessions and live by the alms and food given to them by the local population. They do not beg, but rather are given the means to live by people for whom this is the right way to behave and which brings them merit in their lives

Symbols

The symbol of the ever turning eight-spoked **Wheel of Law** represents the important Middle Way taught by the Buddha and the ever-turning and changing nature of life. The **lotus flower** is a key symbol of good fortune and progress. The **Bodhi Tree** has significance because it was under this tree that the Buddha sat for his three nights of deep contemplation.

The Buddhist Wheel of Law

Ritual and ceremony

Ceremonies tend to vary according to the particular Buddhist tradition and the cultural tradition of the country in which the ceremony takes place. The following are only a very general guide.

NAMING AND INITIATION

At the birth of a new baby, a monk will come to the house to chant and bless the baby. In one branch of Buddhism the monk will return when the baby is one month old to tie sacred threads around the baby's wrist, which will welcome a spirit to protect the child.

The only Buddhist initiation ceremony is held before entering a monastery to train as a monk or nun. Many more boys than girls will enter this kind of training. Boys of eight or more years old go through the **pravrajya** ceremony, for which their head is shaved, and they then enter the monastery. However, for most of them it will be only for a few months of study.

WEDDINGS

During the ceremony the couple make promises to each other, including fidelty. A Buddhist monk will bless the marriage. The couple and their families promise to follow the Buddhist guidance for a good life.

The exact form of the ceremony can differ between countries. For instance, in Thailand, a Buddhist monk is present at a marriage which may take place in a hall or vihara. The bride and groom wear embroidered clothes and sit side-by-side on a silk cushion. Another couple act as their sponsors. A silk scarf is wrapped around the hand of the bride and groom and they eat together from a silver bowl to symbolise that they will now share everything. The couple make promises of commitment to each other and may then go to a local monastery to be blessed by the monks and pay their respects to the Buddha.

FUNERALS

Buddhists try not to fear death and some groups have elaborate and very lively funerals which take the last chance to celebrate the life of the deceased. They may be a joyful occasion with music, food and sometimes fireworks. Monks will recite prayers and the body will usually be cremated.

Festivals and celebrations

Buddhism has developed very differently around the world and some Buddhist groups celebrate different days and events. These are some general examples.

- **Wesak** is the name of the festival and the month in the Buddhist year (May or June) when the Buddha was believed to be born, experienced enlightenment and died. At the time of the full moon, celebrations are spread over three days and Buddhists clean and decorate their homes. (See also page 145.)
- **Dhamma Day** (in July) celebrates three events in the life of the Buddha: when he took his two main followers, his first sermon, and the occasion when he predicted his death in three months' time.
- **Kathina Day** marks the end of the rainy season (October or November) in South East Asia and is a time when Buddhists give monks new robes in thanks for their spiritual guidance. (See also page 146.)

Application to daily living

Buddhism does not include any requirements about dress or diet. A Buddhist will wear the clothes customary for his or her nationality. For instance, Asian women who are Buddhists wear saris, but this style of dress is a cultural tradition and not determined by their faith. It is only Buddhist monks who wear distinctive orange robes and shave their head, as was believed to be the style of Buddha's earliest followers.

Buddhists are expected to reach their own decisions on practical issues such as diet. Many Buddhists decide to be vegetarian, but certainly not all.

Sikhism

•••••••••••••••••••••• **A note on terms** ••••••••••••••••••••••••

Sikhism developed in the Punjab and so terms are derived from **Punjabi**. Accurate translation is difficult since the Gurmukhi script has 33 letters in contrast to the 26 of the English alphabet.

Background and key beliefs

The Sikh faith developed over 500 years ago within the Punjab (land of five rivers), an area now in both Pakistan and north west India. The movement was started by **Guru Nanak** who was born in 1469 CE. As a child he studied Hindu and Muslim holy texts. He refused to accept the investment of the sacred thread (see page 37) usual for Hindu boys and explained his reluctance as a preference for a sacred thread of the mind which could never break, nor become soiled or lost. To the frustration of his family, Guru Nanak meditated constantly on the nature of one God and attempted to give food and goods to the needy. When still a relatively young man Guru Nanak dedicated his life to spreading his message of universal brotherhood under the fatherhood of the one God. The term **Ik Onkar** means there is only one God. He stressed the great importance of duty and working for the good of all. During this period of his life Guru Nanak travelled extensively and established Sikh communities all over India, as well as in Sri Lanka, Tibet and the Middle East.

Guru Nanak stressed the importance of religious and social discipline. His followers were expected to pray three times a day. The three most important rules of living for Sikhs are:

- **Nam simran** – to meditate on the divine name using passages of holy scripture.
- **Kirat karna** – to earn a livelihood by your own efforts.
- **Chhakna** – to share your time, talents and earnings with those who are less fortunate.

Guru Nanak stressed service to society rather than withdrawal from it. He himself worked in the fields when, during the later period of his life, he lived a settled life as a farmer. Guru Nanak also started the pattern of the **langar**, or communal kitchen. The aim was that such communal dining brought together people of all social groupings. The langar was established further by **Guru Amar Das** (the third Guru).

The teachings of Guru Nanak were continued and developed by an uninterrupted succession of nine other **Gurus** (meaning teacher), some of whom were martyred for their faith. It is a matter of respect that all ten Gurus are always referred to by their full title and name. Key ideas within the faith were developed through the work of the first five Gurus. During the life of **Guru Arjan** (the fifth Guru) there was increasing political strife between Sikhs and Muslims and, especially after the death of Guru Arjan, Sikhism shifted towards an assertion of the right to defend their faith. **Guru Gobind Singh** became the tenth Guru at nine years old after the martyrdom of his father, **Guru Tegh Bahadur** (the ninth Guru). Guru Gobind Singh became a renowned warrior for the faith. In 1699 in his early thirties, Guru Gobind Singh asked Sikhs from across India to gather at Anandpur for the Baisakhi festival (see page 54). Guru Gobind Singh then took significant actions that further developed the Sikh faith into the form that it has held since that time.

At early morning prayers Guru Gobind Singh drew out his sword and demanded to know who was willing to die for the faith. One man came forward and disappeared into a nearby tent with Guru Gobind Singh, who reappeared shortly, his sword dripping blood. The sequence was repeated until five men had entered the tent and apparently died for their faith. Then all five re-emerged unharmed and dressed identically in new attire. Guru Gobind Singh then anointed all five with **amrit**, a nectar of sugar and water, whilst reciting from holy scriptures and stirring the mixture with his sword. Guru Gobind Singh then asked the five loyal followers to anoint him with amrit and explained that this action symbolised the birth of the **Khalsa**, the Sikh community.

Guru Gobind Singh made further requirements of Sikhs as part of the desire to make them distinct from followers of other faiths within their society. He required them to follow a specifically Sikh code of discipline, the **Rahit Maryada**. Equality between the sexes was required and names were to be taken that removed Sikhs from the Hindu family names reflecting the caste system. Men were therefore to take the name of **Singh** (lion) in addition to their personal name and women that of **Kaur** (princess). All humans were regarded as equal in the sight of God.

Guru Gobind Singh also established the five symbols of Sikhism to be worn by males.

- **Kachera**: cotton shorts designed to allow men to move more freely and to symbolise readiness to fight for the faith.
- **Kangha**: a special comb worn in the hair.
- **Kara**: a steel band worn on the wrist.
- **Kesh**: uncut hair, because hair is a gift from God.
- **Kirpan**: a symbolic sword to show a follower's willingness to fight, but only in self defence.

These symbols became known as **panj kakke**, or the five Ks.

Sikhs believe in one God, formless and eternal, who is the true Guru, and whose divine word was communicated through the ten Gurus. Sikhs do not believe that God has at any time appeared in human form. They believe that as people become more aware of God, their lives will change away from selfishness. Part of the faith is **hukam**, an acceptance of God's will. Sikhs believe in reincarnation and that only a few people will leave the cycle of death and rebirth by finding a true union with God. Living in the physical world is an opportunity to move towards salvation from accumulated sins through good deeds, as well as through the grace of God. The faith is known generally as Sikhism but followers tend to refer to the **Gurmat**, meaning the Guru's guidance.

Holy scriptures

In 1699 Guru Gobind Singh transferred his authority as a living Guru to the Sikh community. Then in 1708, three days before his death from assassination, Guru Gobind Singh ended the human succession of Gurus and stated that guidance was now to be taken from the **Guru Granth Sahib**, a 1430-page holy book that includes writings of the Gurus and of Hindu and Muslim holy people. The Guru Granth Sahib is therefore regarded as a universal book of prayer and its guidance is viewed as if from a living Guru. The book occupies a central place of great respect in the **Gurdwara** (place of worship). The Guru Granth Sahib was compiled by Guru Arjan (the fifth Guru and first Sikh martyr) and given its final form by Guru Gobind Singh.

The **Mool Mantar** is the basic and essential teaching stated at the beginning of the Guru Granth Sahib and the first phrase is Ik Onkar, there is only one God. The **Japji Sahib** is the morning prayer, composed by Guru Nanak, and forms the first chapter of the Guru Granth Sahib. The **Kirtan Sohila** is the evening prayer, said before retiring and is also used when the Guru Granth Sahib is laid to rest.

Other important Sikh writings include **janamsakhi**, accounts of the lives of the ten Gurus. The best known stories come from events in the life of Guru Nanak and the founding of the faith, the account of **Guru Har Gobind** (the sixth Guru) and his release from prison (celebrated at Divali) and the significant actions of Guru Gobind Singh in establishing the final form of Sikhism and ending the human succession of Gurus.

Worship

Sikhs worship at the gurdwara (meaning the doorway to the Guru) and a welcome is specifically extended to people of all races and faiths, not only Sikhs. There are no formal priests, but the **Granthi** is a person who has been specially trained to read and explain the Guru Granth Sahib, and to officiate at ceremonies in the gurdwara. Worship within the **sadhsangat** (meaning congregation and also community) includes singing, playing musical instruments and praying. Sikhs attend the Gurdwara and some families also pray at home. Respect is shown by removing one's shoes before entering the gurdwara and covering the head. Responsibilities within the Gurdwara are shared between men and women and either sex may lead the prayers.

Gurdwaras operate as a focus of life within the Sikh community as well as specific places of worship. They include a communal dining hall in which food is available after all services. Members of the local Sikh community take turns to prepare the food. The term langar covers the hall and the food served in it. The whole Sikh community is known as the **Khalsa Panth**.

Symbols

The **khanda** is a double-edged sword that symbolises truth and justice. The khanda is used in the initiation ceremony and is also used as an emblem on the **Nishan Sahib**, the Sikh flag and a symbol of the faith which is flown at gurdwaras. The full Sikh symbol includes the khanda, flanked by two **kirpan** (swords), with a circle around the blade of the khanda which symbolises that there is only one God.

Diagram of the Sikh symbol

Rituals and ceremonies

Naming and initiation

Parents will try to ensure that the first thing a baby hears is the Mool Mantar (see page 51). Honey is put on the baby's tongue as a taste of sweetness. The family then takes the baby to the gurdwara at a few weeks old for the naming ceremony. The reader opens the Guru Granth Sahib randomly and the baby will take a name starting with the first letter on that page. **Kara parshad**, a special pudding, is shared with those present.

Boys and girls of 14 or more years of age are encouraged to be committed formally to the faith through the Amrit ceremony, drinking a sugar and water mix from a special steel bowl (see also page 50). The young people are instructed in the code of conduct required of adult Sikhs and they promise to learn Punjabi if they cannot read the language, so that they can read the Guru Granth Sahib themselves.

Weddings

Marriage is seen as a linking of families and not just the individuals. A marriage is usually arranged between the two families who may involve sons and daughters in the possible choices of partner (see also page 15).

Anand karaj (ceremony of bliss) takes place in front of the Guru Granth Sahib and can be led by any respected person from the Sikh community. This man or woman will talk about the sacred meaning of marriage and mutual duties. The bride follows the groom clockwise around the Guru Granth Sahib while special wedding songs are sung about duty and obligation. These were composed by **Guru Ram Das** (the fourth Guru).

The couple will dress according their cultural tradition, which is likely to be Asian. So brides will probably dress in red or deep pink, embroidered clothes and may have mehndi designs on their hands. Men may get married in traditional dress or a western style suit and their turban for the day may be red (the colour of celebration).

Funerals

Sikhs cremate their dead and the Kirtan Sohila (see page 51) is said during the ceremony held at the gurdwara. The cremation is followed by a shared meal in the langar. Sikhs try to avoid a great show of grief since they believe that dying and being reborn is a positive development. Special readings from the Guru Granth Sahib are made over a seven- to ten-day period of time, with the adults from the family taking turns.

Festivals and celebrations

Anniversaries of the birth and death of all ten Gurus are important events in the Sikh year. The community will also have special events to recognise the martyrdoms of Guru Arjan, Guru Tegh Bahadur and the **Sahibzades**, who were the four sons of Guru Gobind Singh. A few festivals are described here.

- The birthday of Guru Gobind Singh is celebrated in January when his life story is retold to the congregation in the gurdwara and hymns are sung in his memory.
- **Holla Mohalla** was established by Guru Gobind Singh as a Sikh alternative to the Hindu festival of Holi (see page 39) that takes place in February or March. Holla Mohalla is an equally lively festival with displays of prowess with the sword, on horseback, wrestling and readings of poetry.
- **Baisakhi** takes place in April. Guru Nanak was believed to have started his travels on this day to spread his message beyond the Punjab. Guru Amar Das (the third Guru) asked that Sikhs celebrate the day to create a distinct identity from other faiths. Then Guru Gobind Singh (the tenth Guru) chose the festival as the birthday of the Sikh people. Baisakhi then became the important celebration of the formation of the Khalsa (see page 50). During two days of the three-day festival the Guru Granth Sahib is read aloud in the gurdwara from beginning to end by five men, each reading for two hours at a time. When the reading is complete, new members are admitted into the Sikh community through the amrit ceremony and receiving the five Ks. (In Britain, the kirpan is usually worn in symbolic form as a sword-shaped brooch.) The local Sikh community will also celebrate with a communal meal in the langar, with singing and dancing. (See also page 148.)
- **Divali** is celebrated in October or November by Sikhs as well as Hindus (see page 40). However, Sikhs are celebrating the event of the release from Gwailor prison of Guru Har Gobind after an imprisonment of five years for refusing to give up his faith. Divali is therefore important as a symbol of the freedom to practise one's own faith and to respect the faith of others. Homes are decorated and illuminated, as is the gurdwara. (See also page 149.)
- The birthday of Guru Nanak is celebrated in October, although according to some sources he was born in April. This festival is one of the most important times in the Sikh year because it celebrates the beginning of the faith, when the community remembers the original teachings of Guru Nanak. (see also page 150.)

Application to daily living

PILGRIMAGE

Sikhs are not expected to undertake pilgrimage since the important journeys are deemed to be those which take place within one's own mind. Some gurdwaras are of special significance and might be visited by Sikhs, but not in the sense of a religious pilgrimage.

Harmandir Sahib at Amritsar (the Golden Temple) was built by Guru Arjan (the fifth Guru) and is the most important gurdwara for historical reasons. It was here in 1604 that Guru Arjan presented the **Adi Granth**. This was the original and first book of holy scriptures, to which Guru Gobind Singh added the writings of later Gurus to form the Guru Granth Sahib. Guru Arjan also appointed the first granthi. Harmandir Sahib (**har** meaning God and **mandir** meaning temple) established the welcome to people outside the faith with four entrances in four directions.

Other gurdwaras of historical significance include Nankana Sahib (the birthplace of Guru Nanak), Sis Ganj Sahib (the site of the martyrdom of Guru Tegh Bahadur) and Bangla Sahib (the site of the martyrdom of Guru Har Krishan, the eighth Guru).

DIET

Sikhs will probably avoid beef and pork and those who eat meat will definitely require that it has not been bleed (in the Halal or Kosher method). Some Sikhs are vegetarian. Sikhs are expected to avoid all tobacco, alcohol or harmful drugs.

HYGIENE

Some Sikhs emphasise that proper hygiene is to use the right hand for eating and keep the left for dealing with personal hygiene including toileting.

DRESS AND HAIR

Guru Gobind Singh wanted Sikhs to be immediately distinct from Hindus and made the requirement that males should never cut their hair. Boys have their hair wound into a **jura** (a bun) contained by a small cloth covering and move to a **pagri** (turban) as part of the shift into being men. Sikh males are also required not to shave their facial hair, so they grow a beard. Men may wear the turban with Western style dress or with Punjabi-style loose trousers and tunic.

Men and women often wear a style of dress that is usual for the Punjab, from where Sikhs originated. Women wear a tunic over lightweight trousers of a similar material and usually have a long light scarf which is used to cover the head. The women's outfit and the men's tunic and trousers are known as **shalwar kameez.**

ACTIVITIES

If you are currently attending a course, your tutor will probably give you a project to extend your learning. If you do not have specific suggestions, then some possibilities are:

- Choose two of the faiths covered in this chapter or Chapter 2. Choose one faith with which you feel familiar and one that is largely unknown to you. Select some of the suggested books and read further. If possible make visits to a relevant place of worship and talk with colleagues or families who follow the faith. Consider the information that you have gathered and explore what you have learned about the more familiar faith, as well as the less well known.
- Take one of the themes that are covered within this chapter or Chapter 2 and explore them further. For instance, you could look in much more detail at naming and initiation ceremonies or the role of pilgrimage in different faiths.
- Take one of the world faiths and read further, specifically to explore how the faith has developed in different parts of the world. Christianity, for instance, has a considerable number of different sub-groups. Buddhism has developed in very different ways in different countries.

Further resources for study in world faiths

INTRODUCTION

In writing this book I have worked my way through a wide range of source material. I would suggest that for project work, you consider the range of books written for secondary school courses, including GCSE and A level. Some of the illustrated information books designed for older children and teenagers are also very accessible and written in an even-handed style. General books on religion are often organised in a less helpful way and some writers allow their own beliefs to intrude in subjective and sometimes patronising ways.

USEFUL REFERENCE BOOKS

Bowker, John (1997) *World religions: the great faiths explored and explained* (Dorling Kindersley)

Cole, Owen (ed) (1997) *Spirituality in focus* (Heinemann)

Dortch, Mary and Hamilton,Vanessa (eds) *World religions past and present*, (Moonlight Publishing – see page 157).

Langley, Myrtle (1996) *Religion* (Dorling Kindersley Eyewitness Guide)

Walshe, John G. and Warrier, Shrikala (1997) *Dates and meanings of religious and other festivals* (Foulsham Educational)

World religions in the *Children just like me* series (Dorling Kindersley)

The world's religions (1991) was written by a long list of authors (Lion Handbook). This book is informative but the Christian bias of the writing team does intrude occasionally.

Series written for students

You have a wide choice of relevant series from which to choose.

1. Published by Hodder and Stoughton:

   - *Learning from religion* edited by Kevin O'Donnell and written by a number of authors for secondary school students. Titles include *The Muslim Way, The Buddhist Way, The Christian Way, Jesus: the man and his faith* and several titles that cover moral and ethical issues across faiths, for instance, *The Road to Somewhere*.
   - *Seeking religion* edited by J.F. Aylett and written by a range of authors for secondary school students. Titles include *The Buddhist Experience, The Sikh Experience, The Christian Experience, The Jewish Experience, The Muslim Experience, The Hindu Experience, Jesus* and *Signs, Symbols and Stories*.
   - Celia Collinson and Campbell Miller have written three themed books for secondary school students. The titles are *Milestones: rites of passage in a multi-faith community, Celebrations: festivals in a multi-faith community* and *Pilgrimages: journeys from a multi-faith community*.
   - *A new approach* series written for GCSE students by a range of authors. Titles include *Hinduism, Christianity, Islam, Buddhism, Sikhism* and *Judaism*.
   - The *Teach Yourself* series includes titles on *Christianity, Islam, Sikhism, Judaism, Hinduism* and *Buddhism*. This substantial series is aimed at the general reader as well as A level study, where appropriate.

2. Published by Heinemann:

   - *Discovering Religions* written by Sue Penney for secondary school students. The titles include *Christianity, Judaism, Islam, Buddhism, Hinduism* and *Sikhism*.

- *Discovering Sacred Texts* edited by W. Owen Cole and written by different authors for secondary school students. Titles cover *The Christian Bible, The Torah, The Qur'an, Buddhist Scriptures, Hindu Scriptures* and *The Guru Granth Sahib*.

3. Published by Stanley Thornes:

- *This is . . .* series is written for secondary school students by a number of authors. The style is more that of a workbook than a reference book but the series provides a considerable amount of information. Titles include *This is Hinduism, This is Christianity, This is Judaism* and *This is Islam*.
- The *Living Faith* series written by Michael Keene for GCSE level students. Current titles focus on the Christian faith with *The Christian Experience, The Catholic Experience* and *Christianity and social issues*.
- The *World Religions* series edited by W. Owen Cole is aimed at GCSE level and currently has two titles: *Hinduism* and *Christianity*.
- Two other titles cover a number of faiths within the same book: Roger Whiting in *Religions for today* covers Hinduism, Shintoism, Taoism, Buddhism, Judaism, Christianity, Islam and Sikhism and includes Humanism in the appendix. W. Owen Cole and Peggy Morgan in *Six religions in the twentieth century* covers the six main faiths. Both books are written for GCSE level students.

Children have many sources of learning in nursery and primary school

4

Philosophical and faith belief systems

Introduction

This chapter covers three broad and different areas:

- Humanism
- Existentialism
- New Age movements.

Unlike the faiths brought together in Chapters 2 and 3, these belief systems are not linked in any way to each other. They share only the fact that they are all outside the framework of conventional religious faith.

Humanism

Background and key beliefs

The ideas within humanism have a long history, but humanist organisations have developed within the last 100 years or so and the word 'humanist' has only been used for about 50 years. Some of the philosophers of ancient China, Rome and Greece proposed ideas that were essentially humanist, concentrating on people's responsibility for their own lives and a morality that comes from within, rather than from an imposed external religious code. Thinkers, inventors and writers through the centuries have developed ideas with humanist themes and pursued theories and social change, sometimes at high risk to themselves. As with any broad movement, humanists are a diverse group and this section describes the main themes.

Humanism values rational thought and behaviour and supports an approach to life that accentuates people's common humanity, rather than what are seen as artificial divisions. Humanists stress the importance of moral values and behaviour and believe that morality is properly grounded in mutual tolerance, respect and commitment to others. Humanists believe that this life and world is the sum total of human experience and all that can be known.

It is everyone's responsibility to make the best of the life that they have, to remain optimistic and to consider the impact of what they do on other people and the shared world. Humans depend on each other, needing a cooperative society to flourish and it is therefore rational to treat others with empathy and the kind of actions one would prefer to receive oneself.

Humanists are intrigued with the significant questions of human purpose in life, issues about how life on earth started or what happens what people die. They look towards reason, experience and scientific investigation for likely answers and value an attempt to remain open-minded. Humanists take the view that some of the major questions in life may never have satisfactory answers and that no world religion has discovered the truth. Humanists are **agnostic**, a word derived from Greek that means 'without knowledge', and describes a conviction that nobody can know for sure about the answers to significant questions of life and death. They live as **atheists**, meaning 'without God'. These two words are sometimes used loosely to describe someone who says they are *unsure* whether God or gods exist (agnostic) in contrast with someone who says God or gods definitely *do not* exist (atheist).

The humanist movement rejects any belief in supernatural beings or forces outside human experience. Humans are therefore responsible for themselves and future generations and cannot look towards a supernatural entity to forgive them, correct their mistakes or put right their mismanagement of the world. Humanists do not accept the validity of special sacred persons, scriptures or codes of behaviour derived from deities or paranormal insights. They reject any claims that a moral code and behaviour necessarily requires a religious base.

Humanists propose that the beliefs and practices of major religions are irrational, requiring a step of faith that does not relate to knowledge in the usual sense of the word. The movement is *not* anti-religious and includes active respect for beliefs and life preferences of fellow human beings. However, humanists object to special consideration being given in society to religious groups or viewpoints, especially when there is no complementary recognition of a non-religious perspective. The humanist movement is, for instance, opposed to compulsory school assembly with a Christian bias (see page 99) and has campaigned against the laws on blasphemy and restrictions to Sunday activities. Humanists value an open society in which the various belief communities are respected, but they stress that such respect must include humanism and other secular belief systems.

Ritual and ceremony

Humanists recognise the desire to come together as fellow humans at times of importance to individuals, family and friends. The most important occasions tend to be the welcoming and naming of a young baby, weddings and funerals. People who are not active in a particular religion may wish to mark such occasions but do not want the words and beliefs of a faith, perhaps Christian, to which they are not committed. The British Humanist Association trains and accredits individuals to lead non-religious ceremonies for each of these occasions. The humanist approach stresses making such occasions unique for the participants and in developing the details of the ceremony with reference to the key people involved.

- Naming or welcoming ceremonies for babies are individually planned and families may wish for a celebrant other than someone within the family. Humanist ceremonies may include supporting adults or mentors who pledge to take a special interest in the child's future (an alternative to Christian godparents).
- Weddings can be celebrated at the venue of the couple's choice, although the legal part of marriage has to be established by separate registration at the local Registry Office. (Couples who marry in church have to sign the book in the vestry, which is witnessed; the marriage is not a legal reality without this part.)
- Funerals and memorial services are planned with the family to help those present to celebrate and remember the life of the person who has died. An accredited officiant can lead the ceremony and the service can involve opportunities for friends and family to contribute if they wish.

There is a legal obligation to register the birth of a baby and anyone's death with the local Registrar of Births and Deaths. Humanist ceremonies are in the same position as religious ones in this situation, since, unlike weddings, neither christenings nor Christian funerals can register the event legally for the participants.

Existentialism

This philosophical approach is relevant to this book since it addresses some of the significant questions about existence and the meaning of human life that are also the concern of world faiths. Philosophers tend to see their role as one of challenging beliefs and cherished assumptions. In contrast, supporters of specific religions are more likely to work so as to encourage acceptance of beliefs and explanations of the complex questions of existence.

Human nature being what it is, this distinction tends to blur when philosophers become committed to a position and are then highly motivated to promote their own view and undermine any alternatives.

Background

The main approach to philosophy in Britain and the USA has been an analytical tradition of studying the meaning of statements and the way in which their truth can be confirmed or disproved. Philosophy has been used as a tool to examine the built-in assumptions to language and thought. In contrast to the Anglo-American tradition, the Continental European tradition of the nineteenth and twentieth centuries took a different turn in order to study human conscious awareness. The concerns of this tradition, involving mainly German and French philosophers, now also engage some English philosophers, but initially the two were completely separate.

Edmund Husserl developed the form of philosophy known as **phenomenology**, when he emphasised that one must start with what is *actually experienced*, in other words with conscious awareness. Husserl argued that, if you experience something, it has a reality for you, whether or not it

Children tackling abstract ideas through their play

has meaning for other people, or exists in the external world. As soon as humans encounter the world they start to give it personal meaning and to interpret it. Husserl was also concerned to explore the *fundamental essence* of objects, what they share with other objects of the same sort, once all their particular nature has been stripped away.

•••••••••••••••••••••• *To think about* •••••••••••••••••••••

It is sobering to realise that, when children start to learn about concepts such as colour or number, they are actually engaged in exploring this idea of fundamental essence. The 'redness' or the 'fourness' of a pile of otherwise different objects is something that young children recognise through experience, or after help from adults. Neither 'red' nor 'four' exist independently of the objects and experiences that give these abstract concepts their meaning. Three- and four-year-olds often show a fascination with testing the boundaries to essences of meaning in their world. For instance, when they mix colours of paint on the paper, at what point does red become orange? When my son was this age he was very interested in the point at which a 'wood' became a 'forest' and what was the difference between a 'tunnel' and a 'bridge'.

Husserl was important because he opened philosophy to the study of human experiences, including the emotions. Philosophers on mainland Europe then moved on to explore the meaning of human existence, self-awareness and self-doubt.

Main themes

The term **existentialism** is used to cover the philosophical position of a wide range of thinkers who would not necessarily see themselves as in tune with each other.

A central theme of existentialism is that meaning can only be found by first recognising that humans are *engaged* in the world and that their *experience* of objects and events provides *meaning*. The assumption is that humans seek to understand things because they are involved with them. So people will always have a particular point of view and complete objectivity is impossible. The existential position gives a higher priority to the practical than the theoretical in life. It values concrete and personal experience more highly than general and abstract experience. So existentialism stresses that, in the search for understanding, it is more important to be *involved* than to be *detached*.

The existential approach is very individualistic: truth must be related to oneself and individuals have freedom to choose their actions. **Martin Heidegger** argued that humans do not have a *fixed nature* but are what they assume themselves to be. In order to live in an authentic way, people have to take each situation and allow their true nature to emerge through their actions. The alternative of following what others expect of one leads to an attempt to escape from one's true self.

Jean-Paul Sartre stressed that, when individuals operate within a social or occupational role in their life, they are not engaged with their whole and real self. In order to be authentic, it is necessary to act in a way that reflects self-awareness and an acknowledgement of personal freedom. Relationships with others are a way of expressing one's true nature. Sartre argued that people were not totally controlled by their responsibilities but an awareness of such personal freedom could be experienced as disorienting.

The existential tradition led to further explorations of how *meaning* was always embedded in *context*. **Structuralist** approaches developed in the social sciences which stressed that genuine meaning could only be found through study of the context in which communication or actions occurred. **Jacques Derrida** was influential in promoting the process of **deconstruction**, that of stripping bare an event or a piece of writing in order to reveal the structure of assumptions and finally reach what is unique about it. This approach led to the **constructivist** tradition that has strongly influenced work in early years. The main theme in this approach is that children construct their own reality from their own unique experience and then use this perspective to deal with further experiences. This active process requires that helpful adults offer information and potential experiences in such a way that children can integrate them into their unique view, rather than being required to learn in the same way as others in a group of a similar age.

New Age movements

Groups loosely classified as New Age cover a wide variety of beliefs, interests and practices. However, some relatively common themes within New Age movements include:

- Focus on **spiritual revival** and **personal discovery**, with the conviction that this development does *not* have to occur within the existing major world faiths. Frustration is also sometimes focused on what is seen to be a heavy weight of dogma and religious bureaucracy directing attention away from the original faith messages.

- Movement away from materialism and away from an over-emphasis on the rational which is detrimental to the emotional and spiritual side of human nature and development.
- Exploration of phenomena beyond one's normal, daily experiences. An interest in the paranormal takes many different routes.
- Frustration with the perceived limits of the dominant Judaeo-Christian religious traditions of the Western world, including sometimes what is seen as a negative view of the female half of the population.
- Openness to what are for Europeans the culturally less traditional sources of spiritual enlightenment, either through exploring Eastern traditions of faith and personal discovery or in the rediscovery of pre-Christian European religious belief and practice.
- Serious concern about the dangers of twentieth-century materialism, the destruction of the environment and the disconnectedness of most people from the natural world.

Individuals and groups who would regard themselves as committed to a New Age outlook are, nevertheless, a highly diverse part of the population. This section covers some of the beliefs and practices. However, you should exercise exactly the same caution in discussing 'New Age' movements as you would in talking about 'Christians' or 'Hindus'. You cannot generalise and must recognise that there are a variety of groups in any belief system.

New Age movements and astrology

THE DAWNING OF THE AGE OF AQUARIUS

The meaning of New Age relates to astrological beliefs and practice. The form of astrology most common in the Western hemisphere is based in a solar tradition. As well as the impact of the sun and stars on individual lives, astrology recognises the importance of broad eras spanning approximately 2000 years each time. These eras, or **Ages**, are affected by the precession of the **equinoxes**, a term referring to the constellation in which the sun appears to lie at the spring equinox (21st March in the Western calendar).

The Earth spins on its axis but, like a spinning top, this axis does not point in a constant direction. Until relatively recent historical time, at the spring equinox the sun appeared to lie in the constellation (group of stars) of Pisces (the fish). By the middle of the twentieth century (there is some debate about exactly when), the sun appeared to lie in the constellation of

Aquarius. The precession of the equinoxes is an astronomical event, which can, therefore, be observed. Astrologers interpret this event in terms of Ages so that, whilst the previous Age was that of Pisces, we are now in the Age of Aquarius (the water carrier). Estimates vary as to when the shift occurred: the earliest place the change within the nineteenth century and the later within the twentieth.

The onset of a new Age is believed to bring about an overall shift in the quality and orientation of life on earth, as the forces embodied in the sign of the Age become powerful, shaping broad movements and the dominant symbolism of the times. All new Ages are believed to bring a spiritual awakening, because each precession brings a significant shift as other myths and symbols come to the foreground of human experience. For instance, in astrological terms everyone born within a 25-year span from the 1940s to the 1960s had a particular aspect in their individual birth chart, a sextile (conjunction) of Neptune (bringing self-refinement and spiritual development) and Pluto (bringing a slow, sub-conscious but inevitable transformational change). This connection was weak for individuals, but strong as a global influence, when all the growing population shared an aspect motivating them to break down the traditional patterns of behaviour.

The characteristics of any Age are determined by the dominant constellation and its opposite sign, which provides the counterbalance. The Age of Pisces, a water sign, was characterised by emotion, responsiveness, the importance of image and by flexibility. Pisces was essentially a values-driven Age in which the downside was that emotions tended to be out of control and there was persecution. The opposite sign to Pisces is Virgo (the Virgin). Those who believe the astrological basis to Ages point to the dominance in early Christian belief of the fish as a symbol, to the words of Jesus Christ to his followers of 'I will make you fishers of men' and to the power of beliefs about the Virgin Mary, reflecting the counterbalance from Virgo.

The Age of Aquarius brings the characteristics of this air sign. Aquarius embodies rationality, it is the law-maker, with a very broad remit, strong on communication and with a humanitarian outlook. The drawback to Aquarius is illustrated by something that is often said of individuals born under the sign; that these people are most likely to devote themselves to the well-being of society as a whole, whilst their own family starves. Whereas Pisces was a responsive Age, waiting to react, Aquarius is proactive, going out to meet experience, perhaps hypercommunicative. The Age of Aquarius has an essential tension between order and chaos and this is a problem since both need to be embraced at the same time. The current scientific interest in chaos theory and of the concept of a natural chaos bounded in stability is seen as a typical concern for this Age. The counterbalance to Aquarius is Leo (the Lion) which brings the quality of active leadership to the Age. These two signs are not as opposite in nature as were Pisces and Virgo, but they can bring the drawback of imposed order (Leo) which is justified as for 'your own good' (Aquarius).

The primary interests of movements that fall under the umbrella of New Age are so varied that there would be no sense in talking about a 'New Age religion'. Some of the main areas of interest within New Age movements are described in the following sections.

Interest in non-western faiths and philosophies

One strong source, developing through the 1960s and 70s, was in Eastern philosophies and religions. Many people travelled to India and the Far East in order to experience first hand what was perceived as a different and, in some cases, more spiritual experience than was offered by Western faith, specifically Christianity. Some people committed fully to other faiths such as Hinduism or Buddhism. However, some were more interested in mental and physical disciplines, such as meditation and the different kinds of yoga, in order to extend spiritual understanding and bodily awareness.

SHARED THEMES IN DIFFERENT FAITHS

There has been a strong interest in common themes within many of the world faiths and a motivation to explore personal spiritual enlightenment. People have wished to transcend what are seen as the artificial barriers of established world faiths. A sense of the sacred, the power of symbolism, spiritual growth through bodily and mental discipline are all seen to cross over the institutional boundaries of separate religions.

A revival of interest in pilgrimage is one example of cross-faith explorations. Some people make the effort to visit different sacred sites around the world and to approach with reverence rather than as a tourist. A similar commitment can be seen to activities like travelling to sacred sites in Britain, such as Stonehenge or in walking the ley lines, which are believed to be invisible lines of psychic power that route through the landscape of the country.

Some important sites for New Age movements are also significant for Christians. For instance, Glastonbury is the focus of celebration at the summer and winter solstice and of great importance because ley lines cross at this site. However, some Christians also revere Glastonbury, believing that Joseph of Arimathea visited Britain at this spot. Joseph is an important figure because he provided the tomb for Jesus' body after the crucifixion and is believed by some to be a member of Jesus' earthly family, probably his uncle. For one example of spiritual exploration that crosses faith boundaries you could read Jennifer Westwood's *Sacred journeys: paths for the new pilgrim* (Gaia Books Ltd, 1997).

Sometimes it has been individual thinkers and writers who work to bring together key themes of shared human concerns. However, some movements, such as the **Unitarian Church**, have the explicit aim of building links between people of different faiths or no specific faith at all. **Unitarianism** was a movement of Christian religious dissent that started in the sixteenth century. It is now a broad tradition that follows an ethical belief in one supreme God while wishing to involve the full range of any local community. Unitarian ministers are, for instance, usually very willing to perform mixed-faith religious ceremonies.

The Celtic revival

Some New Age interests in Britain have focused on beliefs and practices from lands and societies that are very distant. However, an equally strong theme has been the rediscovery of ancient European Celtic beliefs and practices that predate the missionary influence of Christianity. One of the underlying reasons for the Celtic revival is the desire for a sense of ethnic and spiritual identity that is essentially British. A renewed broader national awareness in Ireland, Wales and Scotland has also sometimes motivated a wish to rediscover ancient traditions. Another reason derives from the respect and active recognition that appears to have been given to women in this religious tradition. Celtic Christianity appears to have had a specific character for a considerable amount of time. Then over the centuries, ancient Celtic traditions and saints were absorbed into mainstream Christianity.

Some people are especially interested in the sacred sites and structures that still exist around England, Wales, Scotland and Ireland. The solar and more general astronomical significance of sets of standing stones (Stonehenge is just the best known of a number of such sites) arouses interest in lost knowledge. A challenge is posed to the view that human progress in skills or insights is simplistically linear, that is to say that humankind today must possess a superior sum of knowledge than any society in the past. Interpretation of some ancient sites suggests a wealth of lost knowledge.

DRUIDERY AND WICCA

The revival of Celtic traditions has led to an interest and commitment to Druidery and Wicca, separate although related manifestations of pre-Christian Celtic faith. The two appear to have coexisted in ancient Britain in what has been described as a brother and sister relationship. Both faiths gave active recognition to women as well as men, both as religious leaders and as deities revered in the faiths. The gods and goddesses significant in the faith were often, over time, subsumed under Christian names and practices and sacred sites came to be given a Christian symbolism and meaning. Both Druidery and Wicca combine a wish to rediscover the ancient, almost lost, traditions, to relearn and develop them in response to modern needs.

The faith represented in Druidery has links with early Christianity in Britain and it seems very likely that some of the first Christian priests were also Druids. The first Druids appear to have had both male and female priests and what is known of ancient Celtic law and society suggests a measure of equality between the sexes. The eighteenth-century revival of the faith echoed the social customs of the era by restricting leadership to males. However, more recent developments have returned to greater equality. The revival of the Druid tradition in Wales led to the renewal of the **Eisteddfod**, a cultural festival and annual gathering of the bards.

The word Druid seems to mean 'one with knowledge of the trees', especially the oak, a tree that has special significance but which may also act as symbol for all trees. Druids use the symbol of the circle to show the vital link between humans and the natural world, a link that should not be broken. They acknowledge the sacredness of specific sites that help to symbolise and maintain the continuous links between people and the earth. Druidery sees the dangers of the disconnectedness of modern society and the loss of the connection to the continuous cycle of life. There is an attempt to understand the purpose of life through the spirit of continued journey. This cycle is believed to be maintained through the spirit of place, of time, the cultural life-stream of the tribe and the genetic life-stream of ancestors.

Wicca is an ancient, nature-based Celtic religion, linked with reverence for the moon and lunar cycles, in contrast with Druidery which has a solar focus. A belief within Wicca is that the Divine has both female and male

manifestations and this faith tends to focus more on the female. Followers
value a profound communication with the natural world and believe in the
spiritual potential within everyone. Wicca remained independent from early
Christianity and continued in the traditions of wise women, some of whom
were persecuted as witches.

The modern Wicca movement aims for a spiritual path that will enhance
personal fulfilment and develop psychic and magical abilities. Wicca is a *craft*
just as much as a *religion*; it is also called the **Craft of the Wise**. It focuses
on the use of psychic abilities for the benefit of others, for instance through
healing. Modern interest in Wicca has also been fuelled by a reaction against
the perceived patriarchal (male dominated) nature of the Judaeo-Christian
tradition and its impact on Western society as a whole.

Both Wicca and Druidery celebrate seasonal rites and festivals to aid
attunement to the natural world, following an eightfold year with four solar
and four lunar festivals.

Harmony with the natural world

Systems of belief and craft such as Wicca and Druidery emphasise the
oneness of humans with the natural world. Some New Age movements seek
a sense of harmony with nature without being part of the specific Celtic
revival. The concept of **Gaia** sums up the sense of a living, creative Earth
that is not simply a passive recipient of what humans choose to impose upon
it. Gaia views the Earth as a vibrant, self-regulatory system.

The aim is for adults to act in harmony with the natural world and in tune
with the rhythms of nature and complementary rhythms of human
development. The objective is that adults should live, and teach children
how to live, in a way that works *with* nature, rather than fighting or trying
to control natural forces. Nature tends to be viewed as female, as **Mother
Earth** who will nurture humankind if allowed to do so without hindrance.
Children and adults should show a reverence for the natural world and
celebrate its cycle and rhythms by the seasons.

An integral part of the natural approach is often to take a **holistic** (whole or
fully rounded) view of the human condition, of children's development and
of paths to natural health. Parents may prefer to avoid inoculation and
vaccination programmes for their children and use homeopathic or herbal
remedies rather than antibiotics. The argument is that bodies can be enabled

Children can be at ease in the natural world

to deal with illness and thereby become stronger. A considerable amount of modern medicine is viewed as masking and complicating single symptoms rather than treating the whole child or adult. Parents with these beliefs do not avoid doctors. However, they place considerable emphasis on helping children to draw on their own bodily resources and to recover naturally through a proper convalescence period.

Interest in ancient crafts and the paranormal

These areas of interest are sometimes linked with belief systems such as Druidery or Wicca, but some people wish only to explore the practice of crafts and exploration of paranormal abilities. A few examples follow, each of which are covered in entire books of their own.

- **Dowsing** is the art of discovery, often of water or precious metals but sometimes of objects or people who are lost. Dowsers use tools such as a forked stick when walking in the environment or a pendant when dowsing over a map.
- **Healing** is a craft of supporting individuals who are unwell and mobilising the resources of their own body. Healers often work through the laying on of hands, which is also a Christian concept.

- **The spirit world** is explored by some people through analysis of dreams and belief in the possibility of contact with spirits, sometimes of people who have died from the earthly existence. Some people believe not only in the existence of the soul, also a Christian concept, but that living individuals can temporarily divide their soul from the physical body and experience **astral travel** (their spirit goes to places and sees sights far beyond the location of the body). Some people who have technically died and been revived, later describe the experience of looking down upon their body before re-entering, which is one form of **out-of-body experience**.
- **Astrology** is an ancient craft of working out the patterns of an individual life and that person's strengths and weaknesses derived from the configuration of major star constellations at the time of their birth. It is possible to draw up a chart which predicts the likelihood of future events for that person, but the step of prediction is not necessarily taken. The Western system of astrology is based on twelve signs that each span about a month within the year. Chinese astrology is based on a lunar system and has a cycle of twelve years, individuals being born, for instance, in the Year of the Buffalo (see also page 147).
- **Palmistry** is a craft of divining the future of an individual from the hand. Each palm is unique and meaning is taken from the length and configuration of specific lines and their meetings, divisions and intersections. Palmistry sometimes considers the whole hand and not just the palm.
- **Runes** are an ancient alphabetical system of sounds, possibly Etruscan in origin. Rune users tend to work with a set of 24 runes (stones or cubes). The meaning of the runes is linked to ancient gods and goddesses. Runic astrology also places the world at the beginning of a new Age, that of Peorth, the Age of Creative Opportunity.
- **Tarot**: the Tarot pack consists of a set of 78 cards. 56 cards, the Minor Arcana, are contained in four suits and are the forerunners of modern playing cards. The other 22 cards are picture cards, called the Major Arcana and are said to derive from ancient mystic knowledge, linked sometimes to ancient Egypt but also to China and the Kabbalistic lore of the Hebrews. The cards are used to divine significant future events in the life of a person who consults the Tarot user. A Tarot pack is believed to develop power with use, so the more ancient sets have greater power. A Tarot reader will have his or her own cards, and they alone will use them.

None of these crafts ever disappeared completely but there has been a revival of serious interest within the twentieth century. Some crafts, as seen through simplistic astrological predictions in newspapers or palm reading at fairs, have an apparent familiarity but that does not reflect the complex nature of the craft for experienced practitioners.

•••••••••••••••••••••• **To think about** ••••••••••••••••••••

Consider in what ways the range of interests within the very broad New Age movement link with the essentially human concerns described on page 1. For instance:

- Looking for meaning in life as it happens.
- Seeking some predictability in an uncertain existence.

- Wanting some sense of extension beyond what can be directly experienced through the five senses.

The New Age movements can not be described as religions in the same way as the world faiths described in Chapters 2 and 3, but how do you think the beliefs or practices could support human concerns?

Further reading

HUMANISM

The British Humanist Association (BHA) is a good source of information about the movement. The BHA publishes a range of books and leaflets about humanism, ceremonies and briefings on contemporary moral issues. Contact them at 47 Theobalds Road, London WC1X 8SP. Tel: 0171 430 0908, e-mail robert@humanism.org.uk

Cole, Owen (ed) (1997) *Spirituality in focus* (Heinemann) has a chapter on humanism.
Mason, Marilyn 'Faith and values without God – a humanist perspective' in *World Religions in education 1998–9* (Shap Working Party on World Religions in Education).
Smoker, Barbara (1998) *Humanism* (published by the BHA, see above)

EXISTENTIALISM

General books on philosophy, of which existentialism is a part, can be heavy going to read. Try: Thompson, Mel (1995) *Teach yourself philosophy* (Hodder and Stoughton).

THE CELTIC TRADITION

Pennick, Nigel (1997) *The Celtic saints* (Thorsons) provides a useful blend of history, lives of the key figures and a tracking of how early Christianity absorbed the Celtic traditions.

Wallace, Martin (1998) *The Celtic Resource Book* (The National Society and Church House Publishing) gives some information on Celtic Christianity and its revival, includes some prayers and liturgies and some explanation of Celtic knotwork.

The Book of Kells (1980) published by Thames and Hudson. Reproductions from one of the illustrated medieval manuscripts, showing the use of knotwork in a sacred Celtic Christian text.

Harmony with nature

You will find an example of the application of these ideas in *Natural Childhood* by John B. Thomson and others (Gaia Books Ltd, 1994). The philosophy underpinning the book is that of **Rudolf Steiner**, who established an educational system, of which there are some nurseries and a few schools in Britain.

5

A focus on children's development

Introduction

Whatever the setting, any useful and effective work with children has to be grounded in an understanding of their development. Within this chapter there are several related themes:

- How do children's understanding and capabilities develop through the early years, with special attention to intellectual, moral, spiritual, personal and social development?
- What factors seem to affect the pattern of children's development, with particular attention to adult words and actions? Are there some helpful pointers to good practice with children?
- What do adults need to consider? In what ways do adults need to face their own values and possible conflicts?

Children's development as a whole

Children's development only makes sense when seen as a *whole*. Inevitably, we tend to focus on one aspect of development at a time. However, it is crucial never to forget that children's experience and understanding does not proceed in neat compartments. The diagram on page 76 offers a visual summary of the developmental focus in this chapter. The main points are that:

- It is only possible to make sense of the practical issues raised through world faiths when children are fully acknowledged as individuals who are learning within a social context.
- Few age bands and no absolute stages are given in this chapter. Such information can be misleading because it suggests that such development will unfold in the same way for all children.
- Children have potentials in all the areas given in the circles diagram. However, what they learn and the priorities that they apply are shaped by the environment in which they live, including the words and actions of key adults in their lives.

● Children are busy learning whether or not adults consciously intend to promote an idea or action. What children take from experiences can be rather unpredictable. So, adults have to remain self-aware if they are to be alert to what children have *actually* absorbed from events, rather than what adults *hoped* would be learned.

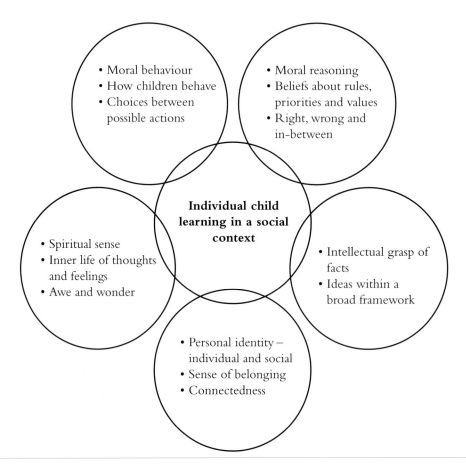

Children learning in a social context

Children's communicative and intellectual development

Children's understanding of religious faith and philosophical ideas grow potentially in the same way as any other intellectual learning.

Information and understanding

Children are keen to learn new information, and their questions will often show you that they are hungry for knowledge. However, at first they can make sense of new information only in terms of their current framework of abstract concepts gained from their experiences so far.

Young children are usually logical in how they think and talk through things. However, because they are missing a great deal of information, they sometimes make mistakes in how they think about or express an idea. Equally, children can also show you the less obvious connections between information and abstract ideas! Their fresh approach arises precisely *because* they are working within a child's intellectual framework, rather than that of an adult. Children can make you think about your assumptions of what is 'obvious' or 'right'.

ACTIVITY

Example One

Margaret Donaldson quotes a revealing exchange between Callum and his mother, which relates to the religious idea of the omni-presence of God. The conversation went:

Callum: Is God everywhere?

Mother: Yes dear.

C: Is he in this room?

M: Yes, he is.

C: Is he in my mug?

M: (growing uneasy) Er – yes.

C: (clapping his hand over his mug) Got him!

(From *Human minds: an exploration*, 1992, Penguin)

Example Two

I recall as a five- or six-year-old having a conversation with my mother in which I was trying to understand the stories of Jesus Christ and how he performed miracles (see page 18). In the end I said, 'So Jesus was a kind of magician then?' and realised from the look on my mother's face that magic was not an acceptable context for talking about Jesus.

1. What can you learn about Callum and Jennie and the context of what made sense to them at the time? What have you learned about other perspectives on these ideas that you now approach with an adult mind?
2. Sometimes children may tell you about beliefs or outlooks on life with 'Did you know that . . .' or 'My Mum says that . . .'. Keep a note of what the children tell you and how you replied. Comment on how you handled the situation. You may have had to make a decision about putting an alternative perspective to children, without criticising them for being wrong.

Honesty with children

Within the early years children usually, but not always, believe what familiar adults tell them. One exception, for instance, is that two- and three-year-olds tend to have trouble believing that they were once a baby, perhaps like their newborn sister or brother. Slightly older children have learned more about change and growth and are more able to understand, and believe, that they were once much smaller and in the future will grow older and larger.

Responsible adults have to be honest as well as informative with children. Young children, even in the early years of primary school, are still exploring the boundaries between fantasy and fact. Those boundaries are confused unnecessarily when adults are unclear in their answers to children's questions or are actually economical with the truth (one argument against promoting the myth of Father Christmas, see page 131). Children need to develop a view of adults as useful and reliable resources. In short, they need to be able to trust adults as people to whom they can turn for help, information and encouragement to support their own explorations.

What is normal to children?

Initially children's understanding is based entirely on their own experience. Their family life, friendships and attendance at any early years settings form the boundaries to their understanding and define 'normal' for them. Steadily those boundaries are extended through further direct experience: events and what adults and other children tell them. Children gain further information from a range of sources: what they see on the television, books and multi-media computer resources such as CD-Roms. Children's understanding of social and cultural traditions, and of specifically religious traditions and practice, is bounded by the experiences they are offered and how these are presented by key adults.

Questions, answers and thinking it over

As children's language abilities extend, they become more and more able to push out the boundaries of what they know by asking questions on topics that absorb them. By early primary school, some children may well be asking about death as well as birth, why nice people get hurt or why some children in the world are starving or very ill. Children sometimes ask hard questions that can put you on the spot for what to say.

In this area, young children learn most through individual conversations and question and answer sessions prompted by what interests them at the time. As well as being alert to how you answer children's questions, it is worthwhile paying attention to the *kind* of questions they ask, or do not ask. If you keep track of what children want to know from you over a period of time, you will find that some of the questions approach important life issues.

ACTIVITY

An example

With my own children, I certainly found the questions about death and dying harder to answer emotionally than those about babies and birth. However, sometimes questions are not what they seem. My son's first question about death, aged four years, was 'What happens when you die?' I was part way through what I hoped was a simple yet honest explanation, when Drew interrupted me with, 'No, no, no! I mean do you go like this?' He then went into a noisy, theatrical death and staggered about the room. I answered 'No', that this kind of dramatic end was not usual, Drew was satisfied with the answer and walked away. It was some months later before he asked searching questions about dying and the tough one of, 'But I won't die, will I?'

1. Over the weeks, collect examples of children's comments or questions that you have to think about in order to answer.
2. What can you learn about how children approach and explore significant questions about how life works? What insights can you gain about how they consider basic religious or philosophical ideas?

Note that children vary considerably and it is likely that you will only gain examples in this area from some of the children.

•••••••••••••••••• *Ideas for good practice* ••••••••••••••••••

- Listen to children and learn from them. Their mistakes can be endearing, even amusing. However, when you listen properly, you will gain an insight into the world of the *individual* child who is talking. You will also be reminded how some ideas are hard to understand or accept.

- The nature of religious faith or philosophical commitment is as much about *belief* as *factual knowledge*. Thoughtful and honest adults have to find a way to communicate to children that some issues are more a matter of 'I believe that ...' or 'I think it is better if we ...' and not a case of 'I know for certain that ...' or 'It is true that ...'. (I realise that individuals with strong religious con-victions sometimes feel that they *know* rather than believe.)

- Giving children access to a range of experiences about different people does not automatically promote attitudes of respect, inter-est or mutual understanding. Information is not value-free and young children will take *meaning* from how you *present* experiences such as a range of different cele-brations (see Chapter 7).

- Take the opportunities for indi-vidual conversations. Four- and five-year-olds become more able to sustain an exchange in a small group, but even an experienced worker can be hard pushed to give enough focused attention to the curiosity or concerns of individual children.

ACTIVITY

Take a careful look at the opportunities within your setting for children to have a relaxed conversation with you, either one-to-one or with only one or two other children.

1. When you are sitting at a table with children and one of them asks you something that is not directly related to the activity in front of you all, do you make time to follow the child's interest?
2. Children often take the opportunity to chat when they are helping you in the domestic routine of a setting. Do you make the most of this time that you spend together?

Children's moral development

Observation of children and child development research suggests that babies are born morally neutral but naturally social. They learn moral behaviour and judgements through their relationships with other people: both children and adults.

Some adults with religious commitment argue that moral values and behaviour can *only* exist within a framework of faith, so that without religious commitment there can be no genuine morality. I recognise that this belief is strongly held by some people, but I disagree on the basis of my own values, the evidence of research and observation of children. Humanism (see page 59) also argues that moral values and actions are independent of religious faith.

Getting along together

Some faiths, or groups within a faith, are more prone to a belief that children are born with the tendency to evil and that adults through socialisation of children, have to counteract this negative beginning. Again an understanding of how children develop contradicts this depressing outlook. Babies are full of potential in all possible directions. Neither natural goodness nor badness has anything to do with the development of babies and very young children.

Moral behaviour of children

Babies and young children act upon their environment in response to the impulses of the moment. They soon learn that some actions meet with adult approval, even encouragement, and some with disapproval. Within a warm and reasonably consistent relationship, young children would rather have the approval and affection of an adult than not. So, as long as parents and other carers are willing to work within a realistic time frame and not demand instant results, adults have a good chance of encouraging children to take the more positive option when there is a choice. By two and three years of age young children become more aware for themselves that there may be a choice of actions, for instance in handling conflict or sharing limited resources. However, for children to reflect and act within a framework of choice, adults have to help them to see the available options.

Research with children of primary school age has shown that they are able to describe many more examples of anti-social behaviour than prosocial, and they have more words to describe the negatives in life. Children are often much clearer about what they *should not* be doing than about the preferred alternatives. Their conceptual framework reflects the emphasis that is regularly placed by adults on the 'don't' more than the 'do'.

Yet children have an impressive capacity for learning moral behaviour. Research on non-aggressive approaches to conflict resolution has shown that under-fives are able to learn and apply specific skills to deal with sensitive situations. Adults have to explain the moral value that aggression should not be the first option and they also have to show children the other alternatives in action.

Projects on conflict resolution in primary schools have shown that children can be very responsive to the ideas and practice of **mediation**. In brief, mediation is a process that uses the skills of reflective listening and non-judgemental questions in order to promote an understanding of the other person's position. A mediator helps two people in conflict to explore choices and reach a mutually acceptable agreement. Children in the later primary years have been successfully trained to use mediation skills to defuse everyday playground conflict situations. (See page 96 for further reading on this area.)

Moral reasoning and judgements

Even young children are watching and thinking, as well as acting. They might not be able to put their thought processes into words, but an alert adult can see the results of children's thinking. A frequent example is how some children learn that noisy and disruptive behaviour brings them instant attention, whereas quieter 'good' behaviour is virtually ignored. The only effective way forward is to focus at least as much on the behaviour of the adults who have created and help to maintain this situation as on what the child is doing.

Children can move steadily forward in their ability to reason about everyday moral issues:

- Young children are guided by the moral judgements of the key adults in their lives. Children will tend to repeat that something is 'good' or 'bad', 'right' or 'wrong' and may even echo the adult's favourite phrases, such as 'You must share' or 'Life isn't fair'.
- With simple explanations and good role models in familiar adults, children of three, four and five years become more able to understand the values that lie behind moral choices in behaviour. They may grasp that life in a group, or the family, is much happier with some give-and-take or that there is pleasure in helping and sharing.
- Children build understanding from their own experience and, at first, they assume that the rest of the social world operates in the same way. Children who have learned to talk through problem situations can be stunned to encounter peers, perhaps once they reach primary school, for whom hitting is the first choice of action in any conflict.
- In making judgements about actions, young children tend to focus on the *consequences* of those actions and not on the *intentions*. For instance, if they have been hurt through the action of another child it must be because that child intended hurt. Steadily, and with the help of adults, children are able to allow for mistakes and unintended consequences. They also learn to appreciate that friends may have been carried away in the heat of the moment and are genuinely sorry for what they have done.
- In the early years of primary school, children can have a clearer idea of how and why **rules** for behaviour can work. They can take part in

discussions to develop sensible rules for a group. They have a grasp of broader principles such as fairness and can reach judgements on behaviour that cover both general rules and the details of a particular situation.

- By middle childhood, boys and girls are alert observers. Unaware adults often frequently overlook the fact that they will be judged against their own rules and principles. Children are unimpressed by parents, teachers or any carers who disregard courtesy guidelines like 'don't interrupt' or moral concepts like fairness that they have stressed to the children.
- Over-eights can also become dismissive of adults who refuse to acknowledge the moral complexities of real situations. For instance, loyalty to a friend may make it hard to take the right action as determined by school rules. Children often want adults to understand that 'telling' as requested by adults can make you a 'grass' to your peers.

Encouraging prosocial behaviour

For a long time developmental research into moral development was limited to children's moral reasoning and imaginary moral dilemmas. The growth in research on prosocial behaviour has been very positive because it focuses on children's actions in real situations and on what they can potentially learn. If children do not behave in a prosocial way, at least some of the time, then questions need to be asked about adult behaviour. In what ways are adults, perhaps unintentionally, blocking a potential development?

Prosocial behaviour has two related aspects of **empathy** and **altruism**:

- Empathy is an outlook and an ability that children can develop in order to tune into the feelings of others, to look sometimes through their eyes and experience fellow feeling.
- Altruism is a pattern of behaviour, fuelled by an empathetic outlook, when people act with a selfless concern for the well-being of others.

Observation of young children demonstrates that even the under-twos are aware of the feelings of others and sometimes act so as to comfort or bring an adult's attention to a distressed peer. The potential for prosocial behaviour and the chance to develop empathy can be seen in the very young. So the main issue is how can adults encourage that development rather than discourage it?

••••••••••••••••••• *Ideas for good practice* •••••••••••••••••••

Research and observation of children suggests that prosocial behaviour is most effectively encouraged by the following:

- Create a warm and affectionate environment in which children can feel secure, liked and acknowledged. Children who feel they have to struggle for attention and self-esteem have little energy left over for the feelings of others.
- Give children basic rules for everyday behaviour, phrase them positively (as a 'do' rather than a 'don't') and, where appropriate, explain the reason for the rule simply in terms of its consequences.
- Create opportunities for children to act in an altruistic way, to help and to make allowances for others. Ensure that the daily routine and the environment make the prosocial option easy and enjoyable.
- Acknowledge and thank children for positive behaviour that shows qualities in action such as consideration, waiting their turn, thoughtfulness, helpfulness or sharing scarce resources. However, allow children space – they will not always want to behave in an altruistic way. A

warm and friendly learning environment needs give-and-take: sometimes children will be on the receiving end of altruistic behaviour and sometimes on the giving one.
- Offer children a genuine choice and avoid using guilt to pressure them. Phrases like, 'A nice child would help me' or 'Don't you think that was a horrid thing to say?' do not promote long-term positive behaviour. This approach tends to induce silence, a grudging compliance or, with older children, the look that says, 'I know exactly what you're trying to do!'
- Set the children a good example through your own behaviour. You can show children empathy and altruism in action and this approach is considerably more effective than just telling children what they ought to do. Children will often copy you, although not all the time, of course. However, you will see examples of children saying, 'Well done' or 'I like your painting' to each other, as a reflection of your words. Your actions should also show that you consistently abide by the rules, for instance, that you say 'sorry' when appropriate.

Cultural tradition and adult moral reasoning

Over the years that I have run workshops in England on a positive approach to children's behaviour, I have become increasingly interested in the ideas that sometimes prevent early years workers, playworkers, teachers and parents taking this approach. I have come to the conclusion that several strands of our cultural tradition have to be acknowledged in order to be put firmly to one side. These are the convictions that:

- Children learn best from being told about their faults.
- Focusing on what children are doing well runs the risk of making them swell-headed and proud.
- A sense of guilt is the necessary stimulus to make children behave well.

These basic ideas sabotage a *positive approach* to children's behaviour. Adults need to be willing to think through why they might hold these views. It is then possible to discuss why these convictions are unhelpful and discouraging to children. Adults holding these views often experienced them in action in their own childhood. Workers can be willing to experiment and see how the shift to positives can improve the atmosphere of a nursery or school class. So long as the encouragement of children is linked to what they actually do, and is not empty praise, the result will not be a group of spoiled and immodest children, far from it.

• *To think about* •

A firm emphasis on *children's* moral reasoning and behaviour risks overlooking how key *adults* think and behave.

- To what extent do you, or did you once, think in the rather negative terms described above?

- Did you experience the effects of negativity in your childhood?
- A negative outlook is not your fault; you will have learned this in your own childhood. But now it is your responsibility as an adult to consider the impact on the children and try more positive ways.

On page 5 we looked at how a religious outlook can shape a society even when individuals no longer attend the place of worship. Teachings within the Christian tradition that have significantly shaped British society, have often emerged in an unfortunate, negative way. If you read some of the Gospels in the New Testament, you will realise that Jesus' original teachings are actually very positive. However, centuries of doctrine have left their mark with negative rules very much to the fore in some areas of life including raising children. Key ideas have stressed the importance of guilt, acknowledging what you have done wrong and downplaying what you may have done well because of the sin of pride. Children are raised and they learn within a social context and, with regard to behaviour and morality in particular, adults have to address the underlying cultural traditions that they may never have questioned before.

• • • • • • • • • • • • • • • • • • • Ideas for good practice • • • • • • • • • • • • • • • • • •

- Be realistic in your expectations of children's behaviour and in your expectations of their understanding of the choices for action.

- Make sure that you are not asking more of children than you would of adults. I am struck often that many adults do not measure up to the standards of consideration, patience and sharing that are expected from under-fives in nurseries or at home.

- Give some time to reflection, both on your own and with colleagues. Are you clear and consistent in your expectations of children's behaviour?

- Have you properly considered how you would *like* children to behave, as well as listing what you want them to *stop*? Perhaps you take the prosocial option for granted, thinking that your wishes are obvious to the children.

- Focus on encouraging positive behaviour from children by friendly acknowledgements when they do something. Home in on the action itself, 'Thank you for helping me with . . .' rather than praising the child, 'You're such a helpful boy'. Look for *all* the opportunities to praise children for being good. Make encouraging remarks as they do something *spontaneously*, rather than telling them to behave in a certain way and then thanking them for obeying you.

- Ask yourself regularly, 'What good examples have I set for the children today?' Consider the messages communicated through your own behaviour: what you do and what you say. Are you actively doing that which you ask of children: listening and not interrupting, giving people the benefit of the doubt, being fair, following your own rules, saying sorry and so on.

- Be ready to talk around issues with children, when they are responsive. Acknowledge that it is not always easy to do what seems to be the right thing and support them in their struggles.

- Sometimes it helps to articulate what you are doing and maybe why. You can share your doubts or weigh up the issues out loud, although what is appropriate will vary with the age of children. You cannot expect children to address and explore moral dilemmas if you act as if there are none, at least for you.

•••••••••••••••••••••• *To think about* ••••••••••••••••••••

1. Look at the Early Learning Goals for three- to five-years-olds and focus on those for Personal and Social Development.

2. Now think of any group of adults whom you know well, personally or professionally. How well do they match up against these criteria?

Children's spiritual and personal development

A question of meaning

There has been very little research on children's spiritual development. Even discussion of the area can be confused by different views that arise more from adult convictions than attention to what may, or may not, be developmentally possible for children of different ages. The different viewpoints can be loosely summarised as:

1. Some people feel convinced that spirituality has no real meaning unless it is grounded in personal religious faith, because 'spiritual' means 'religious'. Hence children's spiritual development encompasses their ability to understand and accept religious belief and practice.
2. Another viewpoint also equates the word 'spiritual' with 'religious' but those expressing the view do not commit to any faith. They are therefore resistant to exploring children's spiritual development, since it seems tantamount to promoting religious beliefs of some kind.
3. A third viewpoint that I have heard expressed, and written in a few books on practice, is that spirituality does not, and should not, have anything to do with religious belief. It is therefore appropriate to address the area in practice with children, but there is an implication that addressing a religious aspect is unacceptable.
4. Some people are undoubtedly uneasy and would rather not address this area of child development at all, fuelled also by the understandable concern that any approach is open to misunderstanding or criticism.
5. A further fifth view, which I hold and which I discuss further below, is that spirituality and spiritual development is particular to an individual and their own context. It is our role to help children develop a view of their own spirituality, whatever that may mean for them.

So a vital first step is to explain what I mean by children's spiritual development and spirituality in general. You may or may not agree, but you will then understand the way in which I am talking about children.

WHAT IS SPIRITUALITY?

My working definition of spirituality is that it is *an awareness of and connectedness to that part of human experience that does not have to answer to rational analysis*. The spiritual dimension can encompass all or any of:

- **An inner life of feelings** in which the emotional dimension can simply be experienced in response to events. For me this includes the emotions of awe and enchantment, appreciation and delight.
- **A sense of the infinite**, of being a small speck on a huge time flow or part of multiple universes, stretching out into the astronomical heavens or into the micro-universes of our own world.
- **A sense of powers and forces beyond human experience or control.** For some people this aspect has a religious meaning, both in terms of the origin of such forces and a conviction of faith that lies outside the rational boundaries of evidence and proof. Such religious conviction can fuel feelings of great peace and well-being. Of course, it is also possible to experience this aspect of spirituality outside a religious framework.

So, I would include religious convictions and faith within spirituality. Their importance for some children and their families should be fully acknowledged. However, 'religious' is not the same as 'spiritual' for everyone. Therefore it is possible, and appropriate, to address this side of children's development without promoting religious belief.

•••••••••••••••••••••• *To think about* ••••••••••••••••••••

- Consider your own views on spirituality and the possible spiritual development of children.
- What are your assumptions about its meaning and how you could, or should not, address this area in practice?
- Explore the breadth of views within your own team.

Inner peace

Young children show that sometimes they just want to sit and be. Admittedly it can sometimes be hard for adults to distinguish between a child who is content just thinking and one who is bored or withdrawn. It may be easier to judge when a child is peacefully absorbed, perhaps staring at a spider on a web or stroking some soft material.

Children often appreciate quiet times in a day, so that neither they, nor you, feel driven to move from one activity to another, following a demanding must-complete schedule. Quiet times may not be silent, although some children as young as four or five years have been taught basic meditation techniques to help them relax and feel positively calm. Quiet times may be when you reduce the bustle in the group and sit together in pairs or very small groups to look at something or just to chat.

Awe and enchantment

Young children are very ready to be intrigued, enjoyably puzzled and impressed. So, much like encouraging children's potential to be altruistic (see page 84), the adult's job is to promote a development that is ready to unfold and to avoid behaviour that could squash this positive quality.

WHAT ENCHANTS CHILDREN?

An important first step for adults is to connect with those experiences that enthuse children and provoke that 'Look, look!' or 'Aah' reaction. Depending on your own childhood, the task may also be for you to reconnect and recall those experiences that enchanted you. If you look at

"Look, look!"

the examples in the box, you will notice that they are mainly drawn from the natural world. Built environments have to be special to gain a mention, like the fountain with coloured lights or the model village.

ACTIVITY

I have collected the following from my observations of children, the recollections of older children and teenagers whom I asked to recall special times, and ideas contributed by early years workers.

- Running water and the feel of your feet in a stream or in the waves at the seaside, a fountain with changing coloured lights.
- Snowfalls, frost and ice, the pattern of frost on the trees and leaves, making the first footprint in a clean patch of snow.
- Little creatures: finding and watching them, holding and touching, watching them grow, like tadpoles. Babies of almost any kind.
- The sparkle of water moisture on a spider's web when the sun hits it.
- The magic of mirrors, including the first sight in a full length mirror.
- The smell of fresh leaves and the different colours of leaves in the autumn, the sycamore seeds that fall like helicopters. Dandelion seeds that you throw up and watch float away.
- At the seaside: collecting shells and seaweed, going crabbing, lifting the stones to see what was underneath, drawing in the wet sand.
- Little scale things when you are small yourself, like 'a park we went to with little bridges and streams', a model village.
- Blowing bubbles, the colours and the wobbliness of the bubbles and how they float and then pop.

1. What kind of qualities seem to enchant and absorb children? What seems key about these experiences? There is no right answer to this question: what do *you* think?
2. What examples would you add? Draw, if you can, on your own childhood as well as your adult experience of children.

· · · · · · · · · · · · · · · · · · *Ideas for good practice* · · · · · · · · · · · · · · · · · ·

In many ways adults need to understand and recapture a child-like focus on newness and freshness and redevelop a willingness to be enchanted. Drawing on observation of children and the ideas of early years workers whom I have consulted, I suggest that the following guidelines are important:

- Be still and be with children. Stop, look and listen with them. You will discourage children if you rush them on to something that you believe to be more important. Look through children's eyes and enjoy the freshness of their experience.
- Share children's enjoyment and show your pleasure by what you do, say and your expression. Sometimes it will be appropriate to reminisce with children about special experiences, like 'Do you remember that lovely waterfall?' or 'I was remembering those baby rabbits we saw at the farm'.
- Try hard to allow for a child-focused timing in activities, outdoor time and with local trips. Children fail to notice and appreciate interesting sights if they are moved around at speed. Give children's priorities and interests space, along with adult priorities or your expectations of how and what the children might learn.

- Respond to and answer the questions to which children want a reply. Sometimes children want and are ready for information about natural phenomena but sometimes they just want to watch the snail very slowly moving across the path and leaving its trail.
- Share enjoyment with children and avoid the temptation to reduce all experiences to rational information and explanation. Mystery is often something to enjoy and not to be unpacked into cause and effect. Curiosity is not just something to be solved by an adult explanation. Sometimes, it is enough to stare up into the night sky and appreciate the beauty of the moon and the stars. Fascinated and enchanted children will be ready at some future date, perhaps very soon, to learn about some basic astronomy.
- Avoid any discouraging remarks to children. Children's delight is easily squashed by patronising smiles or dismissive comments like, 'It's just a . . .'. What's so interesting about . . .' or 'It's dirty, leave it alone.' Issues of hygiene and concerns like 'Don't pull its legs off' can be addressed in a way that leaves a child still able to relish the newness of the experience.

Children are ready to be delighted

Children and religious faith

There is very little published in developmental terms about how children in families with a religious faith come to understand the beliefs and practices. Many books on child development do not even mention religion unless it is within a cross-cultural context, as a means of contrasting ways that families raise children and socialisation. A few tentative suggestions follow:

- Young children tend to believe what familiar adults, especially their parents, tell them. It seems likely that religious instruction within the family or in the community will work in the same way.
- Children try to make sense of the ideas that are expressed to them (see the examples on page 77) and some children are more inquiring than others. Sometimes children may receive what, to them, are satisfactory answers to

their questions. At other times, adult evasions or even annoyance at being asked may sow some seeds of doubt. It is important to bear in mind that all faiths have some patterns of belief that are highly complex (see Chapters 2, 3 and 4), that even adults do not fully comprehend.

- Some adults may explain that religious belief is less a matter of rational proof than acceptance and faith. Children may then grasp that questions about 'what we believe' are more acceptable than questions to explore 'why' and 'proof'. Like some adults within any faith, it seems likely that older children may steadily take the view that some parts of the faith are more central or acceptable to them than others.
- Children will accept ideas and codes for behaviour as normal and right until such time that experience makes them question and wonder. The result may be a strengthening of faith, a partial or complete rejection.
- Religious family commitment may also be part of children's social and personal identity and, again rather like for some adults, the religious component may be subsumed, at least partly, in the positive sense that 'our religious identity makes us the people we are'.
- As children's experience extends they become aware that not every family operates in the same way as their own. In a diverse area, children will have many experiences that demonstrate the variety.

A sense of belonging and social place

Young children are developing a sense of themselves, both as individuals and as people who fit into the social fabric. This side of development is sometimes linked with the family's religious faith or philosophical commitment, involving specific beliefs and practices. Children's personal identity may be supported by a sense of belonging to a community and of being of value to those around them. Being part of a religious or philosophical community can provide children with a sense of connectedness and of 'who we are'. Of course, this is not the only way to support children in a positive sense of self, but it can be an important source for some children.

Religious faith, as well as broader cultural background, will affect how children are taught their social place within the family, as well as within the broader community. This socialisation of children covers relationships, including male–female roles and an approach to religious or philosophical belief, including adult willingness for children to question or challenge.

Children's sense of personal identity can be supported by family commitment and shared celebrations that bring the family together.

Religious faith may achieve this end, but it is not the only route towards family cohesion and commitment. For some children, a sense of clear identity may involve a rejection of others who are undervalued because they are different. This risk is a broad-based one. Some children may bring rejecting views into your setting because of a family conviction that their faith is the only correct outlook. On the other hand, children may experience trouble from their peers because of the signs of their religious faith. It is your responsibility to be even-handed, clear about the ground rules of the group and to address rejecting attitudes, regardless of their source.

An identity in faith

Religious practice within a faith often includes traditional ways to involve children and bring them officially into the faith. There may be naming ceremonies and the commitment of personal guardians for a child. Older children may be given specific instruction before being accepted into the faith as a young person able to make a personal commitment. Ceremonies and rites of passage may mark that a boy or girl is now a young adult and can begin to take on adult responsibilities within the family and community. All these events, either directly experienced by a child or seen through a photographic record, can continue to build a sense of identity and inclusion in a specific local and broader community.

Specific religious instruction organised by parents may support personal development as well as intellectual growth. It will be part of the child's identity that she or he learns scriptures and writing at Qur'an class, Sunday School or special Hebrew and Torah instruction. Organising such activity is the responsibility of parents, but the child's experience may be brought into your setting. For instance, children may express their pride in an ability to read and write in another language besides English. They may share relevant details of what they have learned or other aspects of the experience, perhaps that it is boring as well as interesting sometimes.

• • • • • • • • • • • • • • • • • *Ideas for good practice* • • • • • • • • • • • • • • • • •

- Apparently, in the Reggio Emilia nurseries in Italy, the workers regularly draw in children and each other with the question, 'Have you wondered about anything today?' Such an orientation sums up a positive quality that can be brought to children's experience.
- Despite the pressures on many early years settings and schools, it is crucial not to loose child-focused timing and interests.

Peaceful times, a chance to reflect and to enjoy an experience without rational analysis, are all part of a rounded approach to children.

- Children deserve to receive interest and respect whenever they choose to share significant events with you or the group. Children who can talk about their new baby's christening or their elder brother's bar mitzvah have experiences that can add to the understanding of their peers. At the time, or with another opportunity, it is important that you extend the ideas of welcoming new babies or the shift into becoming a young person towards other experiences, some of which are non-religious.

- Religious commitment is an area that requires you to think about your own assumptions and beliefs and a team of workers needs to discuss the underlying issues as well as aspects of daily practice.

- It is important to acknowledge that other people (colleagues and parents of the children) have different views to your own. They may have firm religious or philosophical commitments when you do not feel strongly either way. Alternatively, you may be the one with a strong commitment and find it hard to appreciate how people organise their lives without such a guiding framework. You will find more about your obligations in early years settings, playwork and schools from page 98.

Further reading

CHILDREN'S COMMUNICATIVE AND INTELLECTUAL DEVELOPMENT

Lindon, Jennie (1998) *Understanding child development: knowledge, theory and practice* (Macmillan). Also includes chapters on children's thinking and reasoning and on the moral underpinning of behaviour.

Matthews, Gareth (1980) *Philosophy and the young child* (Harvard University Press). A reminder that you can find a window onto children's inner lives by reflecting on the questions they ask.

CHILDREN'S MORAL DEVELOPMENT

Finch, Sue (1998) *'An eye for an eye leaves everyone blind': teaching young children to settle conflicts without violence* (National Early Years Network).

Kingston Friends Workshop Group (1996) *Ways and means today: conflict resolution, training, resources.* (KFWG, 78 Eden Street, Kingston-upon-Thames, Surrey KT1 1DJ, tel: 0181 547 1197). An explanation of mediation and application to children's skills.

Practical activities often help children to relate to events like celebrations

Warden, David and Christie, Donald (1997) *Teaching social behaviour: classroom activities to foster children's interpersonal awareness* (Fulton Books). Research on children's understanding of prosocial options and practical applications for primary schools.

CHILDREN'S SPIRITUAL AND PERSONAL DEVELOPMENT

Bradford, John (1995) *Caring for the whole child: a holistic approach to spirituality* (The Children's Society). A discussion of spirituality as an idea as well as application to working with children and in social work.

Coles, Robert (1990) *The spiritual life of children* (Houghton Mifflin). An exploration of what faith means to some children.

Legal requirements, policy and practice

Introduction

This chapter deals with the legal requirements regarding religious education in different types of setting in England, Wales, Scotland and Northern Ireland.

Working with children in schools

The legal framework in England and Wales

The Education Reform Act 1988 introduced the National Curriculum to English and Welsh schools. Among many other changes, the Act altered the approach to religious faith in State schools. The legislation was supplemented by further Education Acts throughout the 1990s and by circulars from the Department for Education. The main points are summarised in this section and you will find explanations about the situation in Scotland on page 105 and Northern Ireland on page 106.

RELIGIOUS EDUCATION AND NOT INSTRUCTION

Under the Education Act 1944 the subject of religion in schools had been known as **Religious Instruction** and it was the only compulsory subject within the curriculum of State schools. The 1988 Act renamed the subject **Religious Education** (RE). This change reflected the shift that had already happened in many schools, that the task of teachers was to *educate* children about religion in general and not to *instruct* them in beliefs or practice. The essence of this approach is that children are enabled to learn about religions and to think about the issues, rather than being told what they should think and believe. Religious instruction is seen as the choice and/or task of parents within their own family and community resources.

Additionally, the whole curriculum was placed by the 1988 Act within a broad developmental framework and subsequent legislation has confirmed this approach. The curriculum is required to promote the spiritual, moral, cultural, mental and physical development of pupils at school and to prepare pupils for the opportunities, responsibilities and experiences of adult life.

COLLECTIVE WORSHIP

The 1988 Act required a daily act of collective worship in primary schools. This event is not the same as an assembly and is required to be of a broadly Christian character, although **non-denominational** (that is to avoid following the line determined by one version of the Christian faith). The worship does not have to be a whole school gathering, but can be carried out in smaller groups and is expected to be appropriate to the age and family background of the pupils. A head who judges that broadly Christian worship is inappropriate for the majority of the pupils can apply to be allowed to provide a different kind of worship.

RE AS A CURRICULUM SUBJECT

The 1988 Act included RE as one of the subjects in the basic curriculum for children. RE must be taken by all pupils, unless they have defined special educational needs that imply some necessary variation, or their parents exercise their right of withdrawal (see below). RE occupies a unique position in that it is part of the basic curriculum but not part of the National Curriculum. This status means that RE should be given equal importance in relation to the other core and foundation subjects. However, RE was not given nationally prescribed attainment targets, programmes of study or assessment arrangements. The Act did not determine how RE would be taught. There is specific scope for local arrangements and the option to teach RE integrated with other subjects, through themes or in a modular form, as well as approaching the topic as a separate subject. The main point to bear in mind, if you work in a school, is that you should get to know the RE syllabus to which your school is working. The following section explains the main variations so that you can understand the broad framework.

THE RIGHT OF WITHDRAWAL

Along with a more general openness and communication with parents, schools are required to make available a copy or summary of the agreed RE syllabus, the arrangements for collective worship and to inform parents about any changes.

The Act recognises that religious faith has a personal element and allows parents to make a written request that their children do not participate in RE activities, including the daily act of collective worship. This provision continues the right to withdraw one's child which was established in the

1944 Act. One of the aims of having an agreed local syllabus is to reduce the likelihood of withdrawal of children by parents who feel their family orientation or faith is being overlooked or challenged.

The same acknowledgement of personal conscience also allows for the right of primary school teachers to withdraw from teaching RE and from conducting collective worship. The teaching issue does not arise in secondary schools, where RE would be covered by a specialist subject teacher.

A LOCAL SYLLABUS FOR COMMUNITY SCHOOLS

At the time of writing (1999) some changes in terminology are being proposed for certain types of schools. 'Community schools' is to be the new term to cover what have been known as county schools. 'Foundation schools' is likely to be the new term for schools that have been known as Grant Maintained. This section applies to State schools under the control of the local educational authority. Church schools have different obligations, see page 101.

Unlike other curriculum subjects, it was recognised that the RE syllabus would need some local variation. However, the main clause in the 1988 Act relating to RE stated that all new syllabuses must 'reflect the fact that the religious traditions of Great Britain are in the main Christian while taking account of the teaching and practices of other principal religions represented in Great Britain'. In practice, the 'other' faiths are usually taken to be Buddhism, Hinduism, Islam, Judaism and Sikhism, although there is scope for a school syllabus to cover additional faiths represented locally such as Rastafarianism.

The nature of RE, like the nature of collective worship, has to be non-denominational, The content of RE as a subject can, however, recognise the existence of different denominations. This requirement for RE is part of the established framework for the subject that the aim must never be to urge a particular faith, or version of faith, upon children or young people. A circular in 1991 from the Department for Education also emphasised that an RE syllabus should not be confined to information about different religious belief and practice, but should also extend into wider areas of **morality**, including the difference between right and wrong.

The 1988 Act required that a locally agreed syllabus has to be reached. The legislation made it compulsory that there should be a local Standing

Advisory Council on Religious Education (SACRE). Such groups were already working in some localities, but the 1988 Act meant that a SACRE had to be convened if one did not yet exist. The membership of a SACRE has to include representatives of all local faiths, of the teaching profession and local people such as councillors. The members of a SACRE monitor RE in local schools, give advice and respond to specific requests from schools about RE and collective worship. They also produce an annual report on their work.

The SACRE can direct the local educational authority to set up an Agreed Syllabus Conference to develop an appropriate syllabus that reflects the nature of the local community, as well as meeting the requirements of educational legislation. The Conferences have to outline the programme of study for children and can also recommend that the RE syllabus includes attainment targets and some form of assessment. The Conferences have a similar range of membership to the SACRE and, in practice, are often the same people. The locally agreed syllabus has to be reviewed every five years.

Locally Agreed Syllabuses vary considerably around the country. However, many have now followed the models suggested by the School Curriculum and Assessment Authority (now the Qualifications and Curriculum Authority) in 1994 and most make reference to the six major world faiths.

CHURCH SCHOOLS

This is the new general name for schools with a definite religious affiliation. Most of these schools are Christian, either Anglican or Catholic, but some are Jewish and there are currently two Muslim schools.

There are two broad types of church school, which are explained in brief in this section. You need to understand the nature of your school if you do not work in a community or foundation school.

- In Voluntary Aided (VA) schools, RE has to be taught according to the school's Trust Deed, which is usually open to some interpretation. The school may follow the Local Agreed Syllabus or the Diocesan Syllabus but the key point is that any RE syllabus must meet the requirements of the Trust Deed. Collective worship can *legally* be denominational. VA schools have very varied RE syllabuses.
- Jewish and Muslim Aided schools have a Trust Deed and have to offer RE in line with the requirements of the Deed and so operate a system like the Anglican and Catholic VA schools.

- In Voluntary Controlled (VC) schools RE is taught according to the local agreed syllabus but collective worship is according to the school's Foundation and so might be denominational.

In any of these schools, parents have to be given information on the RE syllabus and the approach to collective worship and they still have the right to withdraw their children. Teachers do not have the right to withdraw from RE or collective worship since they are employed by the school governing body.

ACTIVITY

Look at a copy of the agreed syllabus for RE in your local area. This is a useful activity whether or not you are currently working in a school. The details of the local syllabus will help you to think through what might be covered with younger children in a way that reflects local needs. If you are working in a school, there should be a copy of the syllabus to consult in the building. Otherwise contact your local LEA.

1. What is covered by the syllabus: in terms of RE as a subject and the approach to collective worship?
2. In what ways can you see that the syllabus reflects the local community?
3. In what ways does it give teachers and nursery nurses in school the scope to extend children's understanding beyond the immediate neighbourhood?
4. You could supplement your work by visiting local primary schools in order to see some examples of the children's work and to hear, and possibly see, how the school organises daily collective worship.

INSPECTION

The obligation of State schools to follow the requirements on RE, collective worship and the spiritual, moral, social and cultural (known as SMSC) development of pupils is monitored by the OFSTED inspection system, under section 10. An inspection team visits community and foundation schools on a four-yearly basis to observe and report back on their coverage of all the requirements of the school curriculum. The RE syllabus in VA schools and the collective worship in VA and VC schools are inspected under section 23 by a different, denominational inspector, employed by the governors.

Nursery schools and classes

Children in the early years should be learning within a broad framework

Children in nursery education are not covered by the National Curriculum, for which the first Key Stage starts at five years. However, very broad aspects of religious understanding are included within the early learning goals for children's learning by the end of Reception Year in primary school.

Early learning within children's **personal and social development** is important because it supports their potential for success in every other area. Goals are set for children's emotional, moral and spiritual development, as well as developing positive attitudes towards learning and learning skills. Children's spiritual development is seen, for under-fives as well as for older children, as being broader than religious faith. For some families the two may intertwine but they are not seen as identical.

The early learning goals most relevant to later religious education include that children should be:

- Aware of their own needs, views and feelings and also sensitive to those of other people.

- Respectful of their own culture and belief and understand that they can expect others to treat them with respect.
- Able to understand that people have different cultures and beliefs which should be treated with respect.
- Responsive to significant experiences, showing a range of feelings including joy, awe, wonder and sorrow.
- Able to understand what is right, what is wrong and why.

These goals for early learning provide the opportunity to address some basic issues of understanding, and ideas of how young children's learning may be supported are discussed in this chapter from page 113 and in Chapters 7 and 8.

Early years settings, other than nursery classes or schools, have often addressed how to implement the government's requirements because of the wish to be accredited (and receive funding) as acceptable settings for four-year-olds. Such settings experience an OFSTED inspection as well as the inspection under the Children Act 1989 (see page 107). Currently (1999) there are developments which should result in less duplication in the inspection of these early years settings.

The role of nursery nurses

A considerable number of nursery nurses work with teachers in nursery or primary schools. Surveys have shown that the daily role of nursery nurses varies a great deal between schools and much seems to depend on the relationship established with teaching staff. Whether nursery nurses are involved in a genuine partnership or restricted to a subsidiary assistant role depends partly on teachers' respect for the training and experience of the nursery nurse.

• • • • • • • • • • • • • • • • • • • *Ideas for good practice* • • • • • • • • • • • • • • • • • • •

There are no special issues in religious education for the role of nursery nurses in schools. If you work in this position, good practice is consistent with your involvement in all other aspects of the curriculum and daily life with the children. Some key issues include:

- Make sure that you know and understand the policy and practice of RE in your nursery or primary school.
- Be willing to discuss the issues that arise and express your views, or any concerns, as a member of the team.

- Support the work of the teaching staff and be ready to share your own ideas, skills and knowledge.
- Be alert to the many different themes in RE and how the curriculum plan may involve many aspects to the children's day, their care and learning.
- Share with teaching colleagues your observations and perceptions of how activities or conversations have unfolded with children.
- Communicate clearly with the children and support their learning in the ways that are outlined in this and other chapters.
- Communicate clearly and courteously with parents, support the policy and practice of the school, while listening properly to any concerns or doubts that parents want to express.

Education in Scotland

Statutory schooling

There are many common themes between the curriculum in Scotland and in England and Wales but the educational system differs. The framework for RE is described in detail in the 1992 *National Guidelines on Religious and Moral Education 5–14*.

The guidelines explain the rationale for Religious and Moral Education and provide a programme of study with attainment targets described from level A through to E to cover pupils from P1–7 and S1 and 2. The three broad attainment outcomes create a structure within the curriculum and include:

- Christianity
- Other World Religions
- Personal Search.

The strands of pupils' learning within the first two outcomes are identical and cover:

- Celebrations, festivals, ceremonies and customs
- Sacred writing, stories and key figures
- Beliefs
- Sacred places, worship and symbols
- Moral values and attitudes.

The strands for the Personal Search outcomes are:

- The natural world

- Relationships and moral values
- Ultimate questions (such as the purpose of life or suffering).

The programme specifically includes moral education as an area to which religious education has a contribution to make. However, moral values and behaviour are not linked solely to religious faith. In a similar way, pupils' personal search over ultimate questions is not linked only to answers from major faiths.

A school's Religious and Moral Education programme is expected to be responsive to local issues. However, the ethos of the guidelines acknowledges the diversity within Scottish society as a whole and stresses an informed, respectful and non-stereotypical approach to all faiths. Publicly funded denominational schools (Catholic, Jewish and Scottish Episcopalian) can determine their own Religious and Moral curriculum, although the Scottish Office Education Department would welcome a programme that develops 'understanding of and respect for those who adhere to different faiths'.

Religious observance has to be a regular part of school life and is expected to be organised through whole or part school assemblies. In non-denominational schools the event is expected to be of a broadly Christian character but with scope for drawing on other religious traditions and exploring broad moral issues.

Nursery education

The curriculum framework for the learning of young children is part of a consultation process at the time of writing, so that the guidelines can be extended to cover three- as well as four-year-olds. The approach to children's learning has much in common with the framework in England and Wales, although the terms used differ. Religious faith is covered within 'Emotional, personal and social development'. The aims are to help children to 'become aware that the celebration of cultural and religious festivals is important in people's lives' and to 'develop positive attitudes towards others whose gender, language, religion or culture, for example, is different from their own'. Other learning aims place this development with the growth of confidence, awareness of others and positive relationships.

Education in Northern Ireland

The curriculum for schools in Northern Ireland was established by the Education Reform (Northern Ireland) Order 1989 and some later amendments. The curriculum established a framework for compulsory schooling starting at four years of age. In a similar way to the legislation in England and Wales the curriculum is required to promote the spiritual, moral, cultural, intellectual and physical development of pupils and to prepare them for adult life. The subject previously known as Religious Instruction became Religious Education and is a compulsory part of the curriculum, as are school assemblies that offer collective worship.

The Core Syllabus for Religious Education published by the Department of Education in 1993 is not a programme of study, as with other subjects and the attainment targets are suggestions, not requirements. The Core Syllabus is Christian and contains no reference to other world faiths. However, the Education Department asked that the guidance material developed by the Northern Ireland Council for the Curriculum Examinations and Assessment (CCEA) should include other world faiths. Schools therefore have the encouragement and option to extend beyond Christianity and the guidance also supports the exploration of moral issues.

Any discussion of RE in Northern Ireland has to acknowledge that communities are divided along religious lines in a pattern known as **sectarianism**. The social and political history of the country has been shaped by the entrenched divisions between two Christian denominations: Protestant and Catholic. There are three types of state schools:

- Controlled schools are run by the local Education and Library Boards and are, in practice, usually Protestant.
- Maintained schools are assisted by government funding but run by other bodies, such as the Council for Catholic Maintained Schools.
- Integrated schools are a relatively recent development in communities where there is a deliberate attempt to bridge the religious divide. These schools bring together Protestant and Catholic children and children from other local ethnic communities. The term 'community-based schools' is sometimes used to mean non-sectarian.

Working with children in the early years and playwork

The Children Act 1989

THE SCOPE OF THE ACT

Any provision for under-eights in England and Wales that does not come under the responsibility of the LEA is likely to be affected by the Children

Act 1989, the associated official Guidance and local guidelines issued by Social Services. (For the situation in Scotland see page 111 and for Northern Ireland page 111.) Amongst many other provisions for children and their families, the 1989 Act set up a system of registration and annual inspection for all the different kinds of day care and childminding. The legislation covered local authority and private nurseries, pre-schools, playgroups, crèches, private nursery schools, after school clubs, holiday schemes, childminders and nannies who work for three or more families.

A FOCUS ON INDIVIDUAL CHILDREN

The Children Act 1989 introduced a requirement to respond to the 'religious persuasion, racial origin and cultural and linguistic persuasion of each child'. Religious faith was addressed with other aspects of background because of its importance for personal identity and good quality care of individual children. The requirement above arose in different ways:

- One definition of 'children in need', for whom services should be provided, took account of children's individual needs and welfare considering religious persuasion, racial origin and cultural and linguistic background (clause 17).
- The local authority has the power to impose requirements through the registration process that support the issues raised in clause 17 (schedule 3).
- One consideration in determining, through the registration process, whether a carer is a 'fit person' is his or her willingness to accept children from a range of religious, racial, cultural and linguistic backgrounds and actively to support individual children on these aspects of their identity and care needs (clause 71).
- One of the possible reasons for the cancellation of registration of day care or childminding is that the care is seriously inadequate in terms of the needs of an individual child with regard to religious persuasion, racial origin and cultural and linguistic background (clause 74).
- The same individual considerations also apply to the welfare of children in the care of the local authority, in residential children's homes and for private fostering arrangements (clauses 64, 67 and 69).

Primary legislation, such as the Children Act 1989, is written in legal language and it is usual that the relevant government department issues guidance, sometimes supported later by circulars, in order to explain to practitioners what the law means in practice. The Department of Health issued several books of guidance on this Act and volume 2 was written for day care, entitled *Family Support, Day care and Educational Provision for Young Children* (1991).

A BROADER FRAMEWORK

The Children Act 1989 established that the religious persuasion of individual children should be actively and positively acknowledged through the care that they receive in early years settings, playwork or childminding. The Guidance and Regulations issued by the Department of Health confirmed the importance of good quality care and early education for the identity and sense of self-worth of individual children. However, the section on standards (part 6) specifically extended the obligation to the learning of all the children, regardless of the exact level of diversity within a setting or the local community. So the Guidance took issues of good practice beyond responsiveness to the individual children currently attending a setting. Several paragraphs stressed the importance of developing positive attitudes in young children, and working against possible prejudices, through the learning experiences, play materials and activities provided in a setting.

The recommendations within the Guidance led some local authorities to make specific requests in their own local guidelines for an approach to children's personal care, learning activities and a range of play materials that would meet the individual needs of children and the aim of promoting positive attitudes. Some local authorities have required providers to sign a declaration of commitment to equal opportunities for all children on the grounds of religious affiliation, racial origin and cultural and linguistic background.

ISSUES, CONFUSIONS AND CHALLENGES

The Children Act 1989 reflected the prevailing approach within early years that stressed the importance of equal opportunities, either through curriculum development that reflected a multi-cultural society or the more active tackling of attitudes through anti-discriminatory practice. Religious belief and practice therefore often appear as a sub-set of concerns about cultural differences, racial discrimination and inequality. This approach has sometimes led to potential confusion:

- Religious celebrations are sometimes presented solely in terms of cultural traditions. Workers, who feel uneasy about acknowledging religious belief, can risk overlooking or minimising its importance for some families and their children.
- The promotion of a positive outlook on cultural variety, underpinned by racial equality, has also sometimes underestimated the depth of feeling when families have religious faith. Individuals of any ethnic background can be rigid in their attitudes and may reject people who are different from themselves.

- Religious diversity is sometimes linked almost completely with ethnic diversity, specifically with a local presence of non-white residents. Yet, a mainly white local population may include diversity of faiths, or groups within a faith, interest in New Age movements and commitment to a humanist approach. Families from a variety of non-European origins will include a rich array of different faiths and sometimes no specific religious affiliation at all.

Some nurseries, playgroups or pre-schools are linked with a specific place of worship or a particular religious faith. Early years or playwork settings, registered under the Children Act 1989, are obliged to follow the Guidance that accompanied that Act and therefore the local guidelines. However, registration and inspection teams have faced dilemmas with settings which resist developments that they believe compromise their religious beliefs and some refuse to sign equal opportunity declarations. In some cases, an acceptable compromise has been reached, but other settings have gone through the appeals procedure.

A compromise can usually be reached if:

- The staff team is prepared to show active respect for religions other than the faith to which the setting is linked and which may also be followed by the staff team.
- Settings communicate the religious affiliation clearly on any material that is published about the nursery or pre-school.
- The setting has an open and equal admissions policy and does not exclude children on the basis of faith (but see the comments below about associations). However, of course some committed groups wish to operate an open policy with the explicit aim of converting children and families to the beliefs and practice of the setting.

An unacceptable situation arises for registration and inspection if a setting refuses to show an active respect for any religious belief other than the affiliation of the group, usually on the grounds that other faiths are wrong. If the staff condemn other faiths as unworthy of respect then the group could be argued to be promoting intolerance, which is unacceptable. Activities or worship specific to the faith may be presented as the only right way to live. Parents do not have an automatic right to withdraw their children from such events, as is the case with educational legislation for State schools (see page 99).

However, appeals procedures have established that the requirements of the

Children Act 1989 are not sufficiently strong about religious belief that a local authority can refuse to register a group highly committed to a single faith, so long as other standards of good practice are met.

Sometimes the legal requirements of the Race Relations Act 1976 also become an issue. This Act does not address religious faith or discriminatory behaviour, unless actions can also be seen to act against members of a defined racial group. (If you want to explore this issue further, consult *From cradle to school*, full details at the end of this chapter.)

The Children (Scotland) Act 1995

In some ways this Act brings Scotland into a position consistent with the Children Act 1989 in England and Wales. However, many of its provisions are unique to Scotland and in some respects the legislation expands on the 1989 Act. Many sections detailing the law regarding children and their families include a requirement that 'due regard shall be given to a child's religious persuasion, racial origin and cultural and linguistic background'. What is regarded as good practice for early years in Scotland has much in common with the approaches within England and Wales.

The Children (Northern Ireland) Order 1995

This Order is very similar in content to the Children Act 1989 in that it includes the requirement to acknowledge the religious persuasion of individual children. However, work in early years and playwork in Northern Ireland has to be seen in the context of communities divided by Protestant and Catholic denominations of the Christian faith (see also page 107).

Just as some communities have different schools for children from Protestant and Catholic families, so there is sometimes double provision in terms of nurseries, playgroup or playwork facilities. Northern Ireland workers who are concerned with equal opportunities, take an anti-sectarian theme that is rarely an issue in other parts of the UK. There is a tradition in the early years field in which the community, voluntary and private facilities have been highly committed to bridging the religious divide and promoting anti-sectarianism through policy and practice. Some developments in playwork are also trying to bring workers together and to find ways to promote work with children and young people that will contribute to healing the differences.

The UN Convention on the Rights of the Child 1989

This international agreement represents the first time that all the rights of children worldwide were detailed in one document. The United Kingdom signed the Convention in 1991. This formal agreement means that any government in this country has to ensure that the laws and practice regarding children meet the standards established in the Convention.

The UN Convention is organised in a series of statements, called articles, which describe the appropriate rights of children and young people up to the age of 18 years. It is relevant for you to know about the Convention in brief because it established a framework for how children should be treated across countries and cultures. The following rights for children are especially relevant to issues of religious faith:

- The right of non-discrimination and that all the rights within the Convention apply to all children equally, whatever their race, sex, religion, language, disability, opinion or family background (Article 2).
- Children have the right to express their views about anything that affects their life and to have adults listen to them (Article 12).
- Children have the right to express what they think and feel so long as they do not break the law or impinge on the rights of other people (Article 13).
- Parents have a duty to provide children with guidance. However, children have the right to choose their own religion and to express their own views as soon as they are able to decide for themselves (Article 14).
- When children cannot be cared for within their own family, the children's race, religion, culture and language must all be taken into consideration in decisions about an alternative home (Article 20).
- Children of minority communities and indigenous populations have the right to enjoy their own culture and to practise their own religion and language (Article 30).

If you look back at the discussion of the Children Act 1989 you will see that some of the key issues of children's rights are built into the legislation. The Children (Scotland) Act 1995 had a more explicit link with the Convention. So, although the UN Convention may seem far removed from your daily work with children, it is part of a framework of what is now seen as good practice.

Development of a policy

Written policies fulfil two important functions:

- The process of discussing, writing and reviewing a policy helps a team to clarify the aims of an area of work as well as the content.
- A written policy offers a form of communication between your setting and other people who have a legitimate interest in what you are doing and how, for instance, governors or members of a management committee, inspectors, parents and other local people.

A policy in primary schools

A policy on Religious Education and collective worship is an opportunity to show how the school is meeting its legal obligations and following the locally determined RE syllabus, which is a legal document. OFSTED inspectors would now expect to read a written policy as part of their pre-inspection preparation. The main areas would usually include:

- Placement of RE and collective worship within the general ethos and values of the school, so that it can be seen as an integral part of the curriculum and not a side issue.
- Explanation of how the school meets its legal obligations, including how much curriculum time is assigned to RE, how the school implements the Locally Agreed Syllabus or the Diocesan Syllabus and the arrangements for recording and reporting on pupils' progress within RE.
- The aims for RE in the school, which should draw on the local syllabus as well as national expectations for the subject.
- Description and explanation of current practice for RE and collective worship. There should be details of how the area is planned, taught and assessed. For instance, if RE is a separate subject in the curriculum how are pupils enabled to make links to other subjects? On the other hand, if the preferred approach is through themes and topic work, how do staff ensure that RE retains a clear identity?
- Some element of future development, since no policy should continue for years without some review. The policy can identify medium- and long-term objectives as well as further development of the curriculum, resources and staff.

Policies for early years and playwork settings

It is now regarded as good practice that any early years or playwork setting should have a range of written policies on the values and practice of the

Policies need to take sensible account of the interests of the youngest children

setting. Inspectors under OFSTED or the Children Act 1989 would not expect a separate policy just on matters of faith, but would expect the issues to be addressed in one of your other policy documents. Some possibilities are to include a description of your practice with:

- The values of the setting and your aims for children's learning. If your setting has a specific religious or philosophical orientation then it should be clearly stated.
- The specific steps that you take towards supporting children's personal identity and their growing understanding of patterns of life different from their own. How will you acknowledge appropriately a child and a family's faith and any applications to daily living? In what ways do you develop activities and visits to extend all the children's understanding?
- How you approach activities such as shared cultural or religious celebrations or personal events such as birthdays. In what ways does your setting show active respect for a range of faiths and for families who have no specific religious commitment?

- How you use the full early years curriculum or plan for activities to address children's moral, social, emotional and spiritual needs as well as the rest of their development.
- How the setting develops its own traditions and rituals appropriately, for instance in goodbyes to children who move on, or facing the death of a loved pet in the setting.
- How you approach the task of helping children to learn positive options in behaviour and to become part of the setting's small community. To what values do the team commit and how are these put into practice everyday with the children? For instance, how are children enabled to share or to respect one another?
- In the ways children are encouraged to develop an appreciation of the natural world, to be able to feel enthusiasm and joy and to delight in new experiences.
- How your approach in this area links with other policies, for instance, on planning and record keeping or on partnership with parents.

Any written policy needs to be developed through discussion within the team and supported through conversation with parents, as well as with any other interested local people. Displays with short written explanations or books of photographs can be organised to illustrate the different aspects of a policy in action and to show what children will experience in real daily activities.

Discussion and dilemmas

Good policies, however carefully worded, are unlikely to cover all eventualities. Furthermore, potentially conflicting implications of different policies can sometimes lead a team to feel that whatever they do will be wrong. Good practice in any setting is that discussions take place within the team, so that any issues can be handled in a timely fashion and with respect.

For instance, a dilemma sometimes arises between a policy on equal opportunities on gender and one on respect for parents' views through partnership. Some parents, for religious or cultural reasons, want their boys and girls treated differently. Dilemmas also arise over parents' preferences about appropriate discipline, which may be supported by religious beliefs or cultural traditions. The English culture has, for instance, a long tradition of hitting children, which some parents may support additionally by religious ideas.

Such dilemmas have to be resolved through a combination of clear communication within the team, between workers and parents and honesty about what is and what is not negotiable in your setting. A team in any setting needs opportunities to discuss any confusions or disagreements that arise through conversations with parents, or for that matter from lack of agreement within the team.

Key issues in good practice

A range of important practice issues are common across settings within early years care, pre-school education, playwork and primary schools. The appropriate approach will vary in detail depending on the age of the children, but the following issues are consistent.

Understanding and respect for beliefs

Workers in early years education and care or playwork are not being asked to promote specific religious or philosophical beliefs. This form of instruction and communication of specific values is the role of parents in family time. Key issues in practice include:

- Workers are expected to show active respect to all children and their parents. Unless this whole issue is discussed and explored carefully, then early years settings and schools risk implicitly promoting one faith. See, for instance, the discussion about celebrations on page 123 and good practice in personal care on page 170.
- The major world faiths and other faiths covered by this book are underpinned by beliefs, often strongly held beliefs. In order to understand different religions and to support and respect children from a range of backgrounds, practitioners have to know about and understand (but not necessarily agree with) the key beliefs of a range of faiths and their implications for daily life.
- Parents who do not actively follow a particular faith can still have strong beliefs that influence their family and other decisions. They may be raising their children with clear moral values and within a code of how to behave towards others. It is disrespectful to assume that families with no specific religious beliefs have no moral values to guide their decisions.
- Respect is also shown through an active attempt to understand any requests that parents make based on religious beliefs. If the setting genuinely cannot meet parents' requests, then you should be honest and seek a compromise, if possible. The range of activities and celebrations in your setting show that you value all world faiths and that you are not behaving as if one religion is more important or true than any other.

You are not expected to be an expert on all the major world religions. However, as with any other aspect of good practice, you are expected to continue to learn and to be aware of the gaps in what you know. In the same way that you should encourage the children to find out something they do not know, you also need to be ready to check your understanding and challenge any of your own assumptions. You, or your colleagues, will sometimes be mistaken about the underlying significance of a celebration or the reason for particular cultural practices with a religious origin.

If you keep an open mind and absorb new knowledge and ideas, you will extend your learning about faiths that are unfamiliar to you. You are also very likely to learn more about the religious faith that is most familiar to you. You may never have thought much about the faith in which you were raised or which you still practise. When faith is part of your childhood or your normal adult life, it can be difficult to step back from beliefs and practice that seem very ordinary and part of your everyday experience. Religions are definitely not interchangeable, but there are many shared themes of human concern and needs. Learning about less familiar faiths can enable you to look afresh at the familiar one and perhaps to understand, 'Oh, that's why we do that'. This opportunity to continue to learn applies whatever the faith that is most familiar to you.

Uncompromising beliefs

It is undoubtedly the case that part of some people's strongly held religious belief is that they are definitely right and anyone who does not share their exact beliefs is definitely wrong. Refusal to compromise in this way is not limited to religious faith; some political or philosophical beliefs can be utterly unbending.

Within most of the major world religions, there are some groups who are more dogmatic and unwilling to compromise than others. This situation can complicate good practice in early years, playwork or school settings. Respect for individuals' beliefs should not extend to allowing them to impose those beliefs on others in the setting, whether that individual is a child, worker, volunteer or parent.

Most early years, playwork or school settings have no definite religious affiliation. All parents, workers and volunteers need to understand the implications of the relevant policy in practice. They have the right to their own beliefs and the setting will show respect and an attempt to be flexible over any religious practice requests. However, with that right comes the responsibility to show respect in their turn and not to tell the children that only one faith is true or sensible. (The situation of settings with a specific religious affiliation was discussed on page 110.)

Children's learning

When workers in early years care, education and playwork explore religious ideas and practice they are sometimes concerned about the potential size of the topic and the complexity of some of the ideas. You may yourself be wondering, 'Am I expected to tell young children all about religions?' or 'What if I don't fully understand the ideas I'm supposed to get across?'.

It is important to see children's learning about faiths as part of their *whole* development (see Chapter 5) stretching into the future. You want to stimulate their curiosity and interest and to introduce ideas as well as knowledge, to which they will return in different ways as they get older. You can open up possibilities for children when you introduce new ideas and give them a range of experiences relevant to different faiths. You are certainly not responsible for telling or showing them everything all at once.

It may help if you recall how you support children to learn in other areas of your work with them. For example, you are certainly not trying to show everything there is to know about mathematical understanding or cover every kind of scientific investigations the first time you introduce a basic idea to a young child. You introduce simple ideas, encourage children to explore through doing, support them to ask questions and hopefully stimulate an interest in what will later become a larger area of knowledge.

If you work in an ethnically diverse area, you may have children attending your setting whose families follow a number of different world religions. Such diversity brings with it the advantage of many local resources to help you explore different faiths. There is a chance that some families will be able and willing to support activities within your setting. However, you should not restrict yourself only to those faiths that are represented in your current group, any more than you would restrict yourself to one faith if there was no apparent variety in your area. Good practice is to aim to extend the learning of all the children.

Young children are developing their views on moral and spiritual issues just as they are learning attitudes about other aspects of social relationships and how people should behave. It is not your job to tell children what they should believe or feel about religious or cultural events. However, making information available to children is not the same as 'indoctrinating them'. Children will learn attitudes towards different faiths and religious practices whether adults believe they are influencing children or not. If your setting makes no efforts beyond celebrating what the staff team view as the 'normal' festivals, from a single faith, you are effectively telling the children that this faith is the one that matters.

Partnership with parents

Talk with parents about children's physical needs as well as other learning

Good practice with regard to families' religious belief and cultural traditions should be grounded in general good communication with parents and respect for their perspective. Good habits of talking with and listening to parents will be as applicable in this area as in any other aspect of your work with children and families. Some key points are:

- Brochures and leaflets about your setting, and your early conversations with parents, should communicate clearly how your setting approaches issues of religious faith, personal care of children and the celebration of festivals.

- Any written policies should be made easily available for parents to read, and should be equally assessible to all parents, irrespective of the language they speak. Be honest about parents' rights where these arise.
- Communication of your aims and how the policy will be put into practice will be improved if you provide policy summaries. Also look for chances to create displays and to show a photographic record of children's work and activities.
- Be ready to answer any questions or doubts from the parents about what you do in your setting, how you do it and your reasons.

In your first conversations with parents you will courteously gather information about the child and family. Part of this exchange will be to ask about their child's specific needs as these affect all aspects of care and daily practice in your setting.

- Children's records need to show whether the family has a definite religious affiliation, because this information is an important part of the family's and child's identity. However, no record form should be organised in a way that implies every family must have a religion.
- You need to ask and note down practical issues in how the family's beliefs lead to specific requests about their child's care.
- If you are unclear about what parents are asking for, or there are regular activities for children which they seem doubtful about, then ask for some clarification. Once you have understood a parent's request, you can make an honest commitment to follow what they want, or alternatively to explain why their request presents you and your colleagues with some difficulty.

Continued thought needs to be given to communication with parents, whether about activities, asking for their help and involvement or in letters home. For instance, the head of the secondary school attended by my daughter finished the end of term letter in December with the phrase, 'May I take this opportunity to wish our Christian families a joyous and peaceful Christmas and send all our families seasonal greetings.' Similar friendly distinctions were made at other times of the year when the letter home made reference to cultural or religious celebrations from the different faiths represented in the school.

• *To think about* •

Some workers are genuinely confused or concerned about the responsible way to behave. Others find difficulty in addressing their own views, or perhaps have never been challenged to do so. On the basis of what you have read in this chapter, consider how you might reply to some of the following comments from colleagues. You might also like to return to this exercise and add more ideas after reading other chapters in this part of the book.

1 'How can I tell young children about every religion there is? They'll be overwhelmed!'
2 'The children will be confused when one festival follows after another. We should just stick to the normal events, none of the more exotic celebrations.'
3 'What about my beliefs, am I supposed to cover them up? It seems wrong to have to pretend to believe something that I don't.'
4 'This is all political correctness, isn't it? Like banning Christmas and putting chopsticks in the home corner.'
5 'This is a Christian country. People who come here should fit in with our way. We shouldn't have to change for them.'
6 'I disagree with all this. Telling children about religions is indoctrination, that's wrong and we shouldn't do it.'
7 'It's the parents' job to tell children about religion not ours. We shouldn't touch on belief at all, we should keep away from it.'
8 'I thought we were supposed to do Christianity in the main and then a bit that reflects local families. So why are we doing Divali when there's no Hindu families around here?'

Further reading

WORKING WITH CHILDREN IN ENGLAND AND WALES

Brown, Erica (1996) *Religious Education for All* (David Fulton Publishers).

Cole, W. Owen and Evans-Lowndes, Judith (second edition 1994) *Religious Education in the Primary Curriculum* (Religious and Moral Education Press).

SCAA Discussion Paper No. 6 (1996) *Education for adult life: the spiritual and moral development of young people.*

WORKING WITH CHILDREN IN THE EARLY YEARS AND PLAYWORK

Elfer Peter (ed) (1995) *With equal concern* (National Children's Bureau).

Lane, Jane (1996) *From cradle to school: a practical guide to racial equality in early childhood education and care* (Commission for Racial Equality).

Lindon, Jennie (1998) *Equal opportunities in practice* (Hodder and Stoughton).

Further resources

The Professional Association of Nursery Nurses (PANN) published two fact sheets in 1996 entitled: *Working together in powerful partnership: nursery nurses and teachers* and *The role of the nursery nurse.* You can contact PANN at 2 St James' Court, Friar Gate, Derby DE1 1BT Tel: 01332 372337.

EDUCATION IN SCOTLAND

The Scottish Consultative Council on the Curriculum, Gardyne Road, Broughty Ferry, Dundee DD5 1NY Tel: 01382 455053.

EDUCATION IN NORTHERN IRELAND

The Northern Ireland Council for the Curriculum Examinations and Assessment, Clarendon Dock, 29 Clarendon Road, Belfast BT1 3BG Tel: 01232 261200.
Hughes, Bob (1998) *Games not names: the training pack* (Playboard, Belfast)
NIPPA (Northern Ireland Pre-school Playgroups Association) Enterprise House, Boucher Crescent, Boucher Road, Belfast BT12 6HU Tel: 01232 662825.

THE UN CONVENTION

If you want to find out more about the UN Convention on the Rights of the Child, contact The Children's Rights Office, 319 City Road, London EC1V 1LJ Tel: 0171 278 8222.

DEVELOPMENT OF A POLICY

The Westhill RE Centre has a range of helpful publications about school policy and practice, for instance, *How to write your school policy for RE* and *How to write your scheme of work for RE* both by Geoff Teece. Contact the centre at Westhill College, Weoley Park Road, Selly Oak, Birmingham B29 6LL Tel: 0121 415 2251 or Fax: 0121 415 5399.

Exploring festivals with children

Introduction

Festivals are a part of major world faiths. Celebrations will have an underlying religious meaning, although many festivals have become an integral part of cultural tradition and continue to be celebrated by families who are not very active within the faith. There are many good reasons to celebrate festivals, both from within and from outside your local community. An explanation of these reasons forms the following section.

Why celebrate festivals?

Celebrating a range of festivals can help young children to become more aware of cultures other than their own and of traditions that are not practised in their immediate community, as well as to explore the concept of spirituality within religion. If you work in an area with limited apparent diversity, exploration of a festival with young children can be a positive way to bring alive differences that they cannot observe in local families. All the festivals described in this chapter have serious meaning as well as providing a great deal of shared enjoyment. It would be unwise, of course, to try to explain all the details of a celebration to young children but a few key ideas can be communicated in simple language.

Good practice in celebrating festivals

• • • • • • • • • • • • • • • • • • • *Ideas for good practice* • • • • • • • • • • • • • • • • • •

The following ideas are discussed in more detail in this section:

- Make some choices about which festivals you will celebrate.
- Involve parents and the local community.

- Respect parents' wishes.
- Keep festivals separate.
- Show equal respect to all faiths.
- Avoid an over-emphasis on gifts.
- Provide activities and creative work.

Celebrating festivals can be a positive experience, but has to be organised with care if children are to learn in a way that is respectful of religious belief and practice.

Make some choices

You cannot celebrate all possible festivals and, if you tried, children and adults would become confused as one celebration merged into another. A practical possibility is to celebrate the key festivals of families whose children attend your setting. Then add a few festivals that are unfamiliar to anyone in your setting. These can provide a source of learning for all the adults and children.

Involve parents and the local community

Celebrations undoubtedly come alive when you can draw on the experience and expertise of the children's parents or other local people. Some settings are more able to access local resources than others, but it is certainly worth looking beyond your immediate setting for ideas and guidance. Some parents or grandparents may be pleased to explain their faith and the significance of a particular celebration. Some may be able and willing to talk with the children. Parents may also help you to make contact with local religious leaders and to organise appropriate visits to a local place of worship, especially at a time of celebration (see also page 161).

It is wise to talk beforehand with a parent, or other local person, who is going to speak to the children or whom you invite to a primary school assembly. It is important that their approach is one of 'I believe . . .' or 'We believe that . . .', rather than 'I am telling you the only truth'. You will ask the children to treat visitors with respect. However, it is equally appropriate that the adults treat the children and their questions with respect and do not, for instance, assume that all the children, or all the white children in a group, are at least nominally Christian.

• *To think about* •

A personal comment
As children get older they will use their powers of thinking to reflect on and question the kind of experience they are offered. In talking with eight- to ten-year-olds I have been struck by what they notice and will comment upon, given the opportunity. During such conversations, children attending an ethnically mixed primary school were quick to point out the anomalies in what the staff offered.

The children were enthusiastic about the range of festivals they had celebrated and their visits to local places of worship. They had noticed, however, that all the visitors invited to speak at their school assembly had been Christian and that the head and one teacher were especially keen to promote the Christian viewpoint on any issues. The children commented, 'We're not all Christian, are we? But it's like they think we are' and 'They don't really answer your questions; they sort of talk around it.'

1. What have you learned in conversations with older children, if you have this opportunity?
2. What do you recall from your personal experience of RE from your own school days?

Respect parents' wishes

Some parents will be pleased for their children to celebrate a range of festivals, so long as they are reassured that you are not giving children religious *instruction*. Some parents may be uneasy about celebrations other than in their own faith. However, parents who do not follow a specific religion, or who are humanist in outlook, may also have strong objections, if they judge that you are promoting a specifically religious approach with which they disagree.

Many parents will be reassured by your explanation that children are learning about a range of celebrations and that you are not trespassing on parents' role. However, if parents feel strongly that they do not want their children involved in specific celebrations, then it cannot be good practice to insist in pre-school settings and parents definitely have the right of withdrawal in schools. For instance, families who are Jehovah's Witnesses hold a Memorial Service on the day of Christ's death, but they do not celebrate Christmas, Easter, birthdays and a number of other celebrations. Witnesses judge that the main origins of these festivals are non-Christian and therefore inappropriate for them and their children.

Keep festivals separate

Through the activities on offer and your explanations of celebrations to children, you should establish an individual approach to each festival. You are unlikely to create a sense of distinctiveness if you try to celebrate too many festivals within the year. Your explanations to children should capture the individual nature of the festival, the underlying meaning and any associated stories. You should never explain one celebration in terms of the beliefs or events of a religion more familiar to you. For instance, some festivals share a focus on light in contrast to darkness or the exchange of presents, but there are differences as well as shared themes. So, do not describe Divali as 'a kind of Christmas' (or the other way around). If children make this kind of this comment then explain that there may be similarities, but that the two celebrations are different.

Show equal respect

Experience of a range of festivals can encourage children to respect the beliefs and traditions of other families, but a great deal depends on how you present and talk about the festival and the underlying beliefs. You will need to reflect on your attitudes and assumptions that perhaps you, or your colleagues, have not questioned so far. Conversations in the team are important for you all to explore the assumptions brought to any celebration. For instance, you need to avoid any implication that 'other people have colourful festivals' but 'we celebrate significant events with deeper meaning'. Unfamiliar celebrations, or those from faiths that are not represented in the group, should never be treated as if they are 'exotic' or 'just a bit of fun' in contrast to familiar festivals, which are treated as 'normal' and 'meaningful'.

It is also respectful to behave in a way that recognises the integrity of a celebration or faith story. For instance, the range of festivals that you celebrate with the children may well support their learning in a way that can be related to the early learning goals and the national curriculum in primary school. It is, however, important to recall that the festivals exist independently from an early years or national curriculum. Celebrations with a long religious and cultural tradition should be respected in their own right and not just treated as handy source material.

ACTIVITY

Look back over your setting's plans for the last year.

1. How much time did you spend on different festivals that you celebrated with the children? What did you do within each festival?
2. Are there substantial differences between the celebrations you covered?

If you spent all of December building up to Christmas and only one or two days on any non-Christian festival, then, regardless of what you say, your actions are saying to children and parents that you value Christianity most highly.

Celebrations in an early years setting should probably not last more than a few days for any festival. Young children lose the point of a celebration if it appears to go on forever. The making of cards or other activities can become a chore for the children and if workers themselves have to complete the project, the value to the children is reduced.

AVOID THE OVER-EMPHASIS ON GIFTS

Christmas in particular has become a secular celebration in Britain. Commercial interests start preparations earlier and earlier into the autumn, with the arrival of street decorations, television advertising for presents and the appearance of the department store Santas. Many parents with over-excited sons and daughters would prefer far less wind-up to the Christmas season in their children's nursery, pre-school or primary school.

The problem of commercialisation is not limited to Christmas and seems to be a risk when festivals occur within societies with strong commercial interests. Kwanzaa, for instance, was developed in 1966 in the USA by Maulana Karenga, an academic specialising in Black Studies. Karenga was successful in establishing a family and community-based festival celebration that happens at the end of the year in December and is a specific celebration of African-American cultural identity. Thirty years later at the end of the 1990s, considerable unease was being generated by the influx of Kwanzaa cards, commercially produced gifts (rather than home-made) and ordinary products like toothbrushes being marketed with Kwanzaa greetings.

ACTIVITIES AND CREATIVE WORK

Many of the festivals described in this section have activities that are a regular part of the celebration, so it makes sense to share some of these with the children. There are many possibilities for creative work, games and interesting stories to share with the children. An effective and genuine approach to festivals follows these guidelines:

- Make some choices about a possible activity for children but do not feel that children have to produce something tangible to display or take home from *every* festival.
- Sometimes children's enduring memory will be what they saw, a good story that they heard or food that they enjoyed eating as part of the festival. However, sometimes the children will be closely involved in cooking festival food or making something that they will be pleased to keep.
- Avoid the sense of compulsion that every child must make a card, lantern or drawing. You will lose the opportunity to extend children's learning about a faith and a celebration, if the main message they gain is 'I have to make my diva lamp before I'm allowed to go back to play'.

- Do not hold out for the perfect or proper end product. The most important aspects are that children are able to learn from what they make and have a sense of enjoyment and satisfaction. Young children need to capture the spirit of an occasion, although some undoubtedly will be motivated to undertake challenging and detailed work.

- Sometimes, a festival will best be celebrated and explained to children through the support of a book telling the main story of the festival, with pictures and conversation. When you recount, or read, such stories to the children you should be careful to treat all the faith stories with equal respect. You should not, for instance, imply that the story of the Buddha and the Bodhi Tree (Buddhism) is just a fairy tale whereas the story of Jesus' birth in Bethlehem (Christianity) is a completely accurate historical account. (More about using stories on page 155.)

- When you offer children craft activities, you need to explain in simple terms the meaning of making lanterns or cards and to ensure that you also understand the traditions behind the activity. Without thought, it is possible to be disrespectful unintentionally. If in doubt, check with parents or other local people, or use some of the books suggested on page 153.

· *To think about* ·

If you are a Christian, practising or nominal, you might feel very uneasy about a nursery that made a model Jesus on a cross created from egg boxes and papier mâché to celebrate Easter. You would probably feel that the death of Jesus was too serious an event for handicrafts. However, you might feel happy about a home-made Christmas nativity scene. Such feelings and preferences may not seem very logical to individuals who do not share your faith. So, it is important that you recognise that people raised in a faith unfamiliar to you may have similar, strong feelings about events which are sacred to them.

The information on festivals now given is grouped by the relevant faith so that the origin of any celebration is very clear. In order to plan ahead for work with children and to make some choices, you will need to look at the festivals in terms of when they occur in the year and for possible shared themes. The suggestions from page 150 will help you to plan a balanced programme and several organisations and suppliers listed from page 180 sell festival calendars for each year.

Festivals from six world faiths

Christianity

CHRISTMAS: 25TH DECEMBER OR 6TH JANUARY

Probably the best known of the Christian festivals in British society as a whole, although Easter is a more significant event in the church calendar. Christmas celebrates the birth of Jesus Christ and the festival is always held on the 25th December in the Western Christian Church. However, Christmas is celebrated on the 6th January by the Orthodox Church, which will be especially relevant if your setting includes Christian families who originated in countries such as Russia, Greece, Egypt or Serbia.

Christmas celebrates the arrival of the baby whom Christians believe to be the Son of God, who died on behalf of the sins of the world 33 years later at Easter. The giving of gifts between close friends and family is a reflection of the valuable gifts brought to Jesus and his earthly parents, Mary and Joseph, by three men who had travelled a considerable distance to see the child and had navigated by a bright star. The travellers, sometimes called the Magi, were most likely astrologer–astronomers (the two disciplines were closely linked at the time). It is only more recent Christmas stories and carols that refer to 'kings'. Historical and astronomical records suggest that Christ was probably born in January rather than December. But Christmas was fixed at the midwinter festival to replace pre-Christian festivities held at this time.

The Christmas celebration has many associated cultural traditions that have grown over the centuries. The tradition of rich food and plenty of drink has its origins in the midwinter festival when people needed to cheer themselves up to face the second half of the winter season. The exchange of cards, singing special carols and the Christmas fir tree are all traditions not much more than 100 to 150 years old.

POSSIBLE ACTIVITIES

- Explore and tell the story of Christmas. You can read the story from an illustrated book, for example, Joyce Dunbar *This is the Star* (Heinemann) or W. Owen Cole and Judith Lowndes *The birth of Jesus* (also Heinemann). Alternatively children might enjoy story-telling supported by models, cut out figures or a nativity scene.
- Make cards to give to friends and family. You could explore images that are most closely associated with the Christmas story. Some possibilities are the star that the three Magi tracked to Bethlehem, features of the nativity

Learning through dressing up

scene, the angel who told Mary that she was to give birth or the candles that are lit in churches through Advent (the four weeks before Christmas) as a symbol of Christ as the Light of the World.

- Explore themes that focus on giving rather than receiving gifts. Children may like to make some presents for friends and family. You might also talk about things they could give that are not tangible presents: helping out at home or being kind to an irritating younger sibling.
- Early years, playwork or school settings could also make Christmas one time of year that the children are involved in the gift of time, effort or simple fund raising for less fortunate people, either locally or further afield.
- Christmas is at the time of the old midwinter festival. You could link activities with the changing of the seasons, the longest night and looking forward to the lightening of the days. Children might also be helped to think about what a long hard winter was really like when homes were cold, draughty and there was no central heating, inside toilets or running water. (There is a natural link across, of course, to the harshness of winter today for people with very limited finance and inadequate or no housing.)

THE PROBLEM WITH FATHER CHRISTMAS

It is a good idea to discuss in your team whether you really should have a Father Christmas as part of the celebrations and, if you do, how you will explain this figure.

Saint Nicholas, one origin of the tradition of a stranger who comes with gifts, appears to have lived within the fourth century CE. However, the Father Christmas (or Santa Claus) character within current cultural tradition is a nineteenth- and twentieth-century development in Europe and especially in the USA. It was this more recent invention that linked the giving of presents to 'good behaviour' on the part of children. The tradition started with a family member dressing up for the children but the advent of department stores brought Santa and his grotto. The weeks running up to Christmas are now a confusing situation in which children are likely to see Father Christmas figures in every large store and more on the street with a charity collection tin.

There are two serious drawbacks to Father Christmas as this cultural tradition now operates:

- Adults, who at other times stress the importance of honesty to children, tell blatant untruths and then go to some length to support the lies when children start to ask awkward questions. Lying to children is a strange way to create 'the magic of Christmas'.
- Father Christmas, as usually acted, implies that children have to be 'good' in order to secure their present list.

Father Christmas is not compulsory but if you decide to organise a 'visit', then be as honest with children as you would during the rest of the year. Explain the tradition that someone 'dresses up' as Father Christmas and ensure that whoever takes the part avoids any overtones of 'if you're good . . .'.

I fully appreciate that adults, parents and workers, can become emotional and argumentative about the myth of Father Christmas as a real person who delivers presents to well-behaved children. You will need to talk within the team and with parents, to explain your approach through enacting a tradition and not perpetuating an untruth. At least think about it and talk through some of the issues.

ACTIVITY

If Christianity is the most familiar faith to you, you may find that exploring some important celebrations of other world religions could help you to regain some sense of freshness for the non-commercial meaning of Christmas. In recent decades the festival has become associated with relentless commercial pressure, apparent even to young children through the barrage of television advertising about presents. A simple approach to the festival and a time limit on preparations may help children to distinguish the Christian story linked with this time of year from the hype and to take a simpler approach to some of the non-religious cultural traditions.

You could discuss in your team:

- What are the key ideas and the main symbols of the original Christmas story?
- How might you give meaning to these ideas in a way that children can understand?
- What broad cultural traditions could you explore? For instance, cooking some traditional food such as mince pies or making a Christmas pudding.
- What activities could you drop? – perhaps aspects to the festival that you feel you 'have to do'.

EASTER: LATE MARCH OR EARLY APRIL

This festival focuses on the death of Jesus Christ on Good Friday, which is a day of mourning, and on his resurrection three days later on Easter Sunday, which is a day of celebration. Easter is a festival that varies because it is linked to phases of the moon. Good Friday is always the first Friday following the first full moon of the spring equinox, which is one of the two points in the year when day and night are of equal length in Britain.

The Orthodox Church also calculates Easter Day (or Pascha) according to a lunar system, but does not necessarily arrive at the same date as the Western Church. Recent developments make it likely that the two Churches may celebrate the same date in future years.

In the Christian calendar, Easter is a more important celebration than Christmas, because the faith revolves around the belief that Christ willingly died to take on the burden of the sins of the world. Some churches reduce or remove normal decorations for Good Friday, to show mourning for Christ's death. Then the churches are full of flowers on Easter Sunday to celebrate the resurrection.

Easter is traditionally associated with symbols of birth and renewal, such as flowers, eggs and young animals. Some of the activities have their roots in pre-Christian spring festivals. Rather like Christmas, you could help children find the non-commercial significance of the festival. Easter is largely obscured by the huge variety of chocolate eggs, chicks and bunnies. There has also been an increasing pressure on parents to buy actual presents for children.

Since Easter is not fixed, all the celebrations linked with weeks running up to the festival also move from year to year. Some of these events are also a positive source of activities and conversation with children. **Shrove Tuesday** is just under six weeks before Easter. This festival is celebrated by feasts, dancing and dressing up in many countries. In Latin countries the day is known by the French phrase of 'Mardi Gras', which means 'Fat Tuesday'. Shrove Tuesday in Britain has become known as Pancake Day. The origin of this traditional cook-up was that Christians finished off any perishable stores of dairy products and meat so there would be no waste during **Lent** when diet was restricted by choice. Lent starts on the next day, **Ash Wednesday**, and runs to the Saturday of the Easter weekend. Lent covers a period of 40 days in which Christians remember the time that Christ spent in the wilderness before starting his years as an inspirational teacher.

POSSIBLE ACTIVITIES

- Talk about the Easter story and make the links to the birth of Christ celebrated in the nativity scenes and stories at Christmas. Read *The Story of Easter* retold by W. Owen Cole and Judith Lowndes or *The Resurrection* from the *Bible Stories* series (both published by Heinemann).
- Explore themes about growth, passing and renewal, perhaps through the changing of the seasons.
- Easter is sometimes seen as a fresh start and new clothes or special costumes may be part of an Easter parade. Explore the importance for many people of starting anew, of forgiveness and starting with a clean slate. Children, even young ones, can often understand the positive feel of being allowed to start over again.
- Make pancakes on Shrove Tuesday and explain the background to this tradition. Perhaps talk about why people of different faiths sometimes chose to give up a food or to fast for a period of time.

- Celebrate **Mothering Sunday** in the preceding week. This festival is held on the fourth Sunday in Lent and used to be a break during a solemn few weeks. Girls in service would be given the day to visit their mothers and they took the traditional **simnel cake**, which was usually saved until Easter to be eaten. Nowadays mothers are more likely to be given a card or flowers, with again the commercial pressure for gifts (also on the created Father's Day in June). Talk over with the children how they could give their mothers the gift of a restful day or a treat that is not a bought present.
- **Hot cross buns** used to be cooked and eaten only on Good Friday. The symbol of the cross is important as a reminder of Christ's death. You could still cook or buy some buns, although they are available for most of the year in bakeries and supermarkets.

HARVEST FESTIVAL: SEPTEMBER OR OCTOBER

This festival is a very ancient celebration that took place when all the crops had been gathered. The festival was taken over by Christianity and is celebrated on a Sunday in September or October. Since the middle of the nineteenth century it has been customary in the Church of England to display fruit and vegetables, which are traditionally later distributed to the less well-off people of the parish. Some seaside parishes may celebrate a harvest of the sea. Some communities still hold the traditional harvest supper.

ACTIVITIES

- Talk with the children about the importance of the harvest, the weather conditions and hard work that are needed to ensure a good crop. Urban children may have only a vague idea of how food reaches the supermarket and their dinner plate!
- Show the children a corn dolly and perhaps make a simple version. These figures were plaited and woven from the last of the corn of one harvest. It was believed that the all-important corn spirit was contained in the dolly and needed to be kept alive throughout the winter. It was buried with the new corn in spring to ensure a good harvest.
- Harvest Festival is a good example for older children to understand how major faiths, in this case Christianity, often absorb existing celebrations that mark significant events within the year.

Judaism

PURIM: FEBRUARY OR MARCH

This festival celebrates the Old Testament story of the deliverance of the Jewish community living in Persia through the bravery of one woman from persecution by Haman (see below). The celebration is lively and children often dress up for the event.

POSSIBLE ACTIVITIES

- Tell the story of **Esther**, who was the niece of the wise man **Mordecai**. **Haman**, the Prime Minister of **King Ahaseurus**, despised the Jews and especially hated Mordecai. Unaware that she was Jewish, the King fell in love with Esther and wished to make her his queen. Esther pleaded for her people and her husband granted her wish against the pressure of his Prime Minister. The story is always told with great excitement and it is traditional to indulge in plenty of hissing and banging of tins or rattles whenever Haman's name is mentioned and cheering for Esther and Mordecai.
- Children can dress up in clothes appropriate for the historical period and act out some of the story. There is an opportunity to make crowns and Haman's hat and ears which are said to have been triangular. Alternatively, try a puppet show that enacts this lively story.

Pesach: March or April

Pesach, also called Passover, celebrates the safe deliverance of the Jewish people from slavery in Egypt (at about 1300 BCE). As well as a religious celebration, the festival is also very orientated to families and is a time to share key beliefs and help Jewish children to learn about their heritage.

POSSIBLE ACTIVITIES

- Tell the exciting events of the escape from Egypt. Families recount the story using a book called the **Hagadah** (meaning telling and sometimes spelled with two g's). A useful resource can be found in Rabbi Dr Michael Shire's *The Illuminated Haggadah*, published by Frances Lincoln.
- Buy some **matzah** (also called matzos) for the children to try. Explain that during the eight days of Pesach Jewish families eat nothing that contains yeast, a reminder that in the rush to escape there was no time to wait for bread to rise. A Pesach game is a treasure hunt in which a piece of matzah is hidden.
- Explain some of the traditions that families follow during Pesach. All the food in the **seder meal** (seder means order), eaten by families on the eve of Passover, symbolises part of the story. Traditionally children, often the youngest one in the family, are asked four questions about the reasons for key Pesach activities. The aim of the question and answer exchange is to help children to focus on the festival and to pass on the information and

traditions. You could discuss with children their ideas about how adults can best pass on important family information to children.

HANUKKAH: DECEMBER

This celebration, although important in the Jewish calendar is not the most significant. Early years and school settings often choose Hanukkah as a festival to draw from Judaism, perhaps because of its calendar closeness to Christmas.

In December, during the eight days of the festival, Jewish people clean their homes and the Synagogue. During the period of Hanukkah (meaning dedication), one candle of the **Hanukiah**, a nine-branched candlestick (sometimes called the **Menorah**), is lit each day, using the ninth candle (**Shammash** or Shammes) until all are alight. The Hanukiah is placed in the window of Jewish homes as a symbol of light, truth and goodness. Families celebrate together, with special food, games and an exchange of cards and gifts.

POSSIBLE ACTIVITIES

- Tell the story that is celebrated at Hanukkah. Jewish people recall their victory over Syrian invaders led by **Antiochus** over 2000 years ago. The Syrians occupied Jerusalem and the temple and forbade the Jews to practise their religion. The Jews, led by **Judas Maccabaeus**, finally defeated the Syrian army after three years of war and retook the temple. They found the temple ravaged by the Syrians who had used the sacred place for games, feasting and making sacrifices of pigs, an unclean animal in Judaism. The Jews cleaned the temple but the altar lamp was broken and only a tiny amount of the special oil left. The Jews used the purified oil to light the lamp and rededicate the temple. The oil should only have lasted for a single day, yet, by a miracle, it burned for eight days, enough time to have purified more oil.
- Buy or make some **potato latkes** (the oil contained in this food symbolised the oil used in the altar lamp). **Butter biscuits** are also popular for Hanukkah. It is also a time when rich **fruit puddings** with sauces and trifles are served to family and friends.
- Make Hanukkah cards, which can be illustrated by the image of the nine-branched candle or by the six-pointed Star of David (see page 16 for an illustration).
- Children play the **dreidel game** during Hanukkah. A dreidel is a four-sided spinning top which is marked on each side with one Hebrew letter to give the message 'A great miracle happened here'. The Hebrew phrase

Celebrating through cooking

is 'Nes Gadol Hayah Sham'. Players put equal quantities of nuts or sweets into the centre of a table and spin the dreidel. Depending on how it lands, the player takes nothing (N), half (H), all (G) or adds more to the pile (S).

Islam

The Muslim calendar is a lunar system and the dates of Muslim festivals move backwards at the rate of about 10 days each year in comparison with the Western calendar. A calendar for religious festivals will give you the correct dates for each year.

Hijrah

This celebration marks the beginning of the Muslim year and is a time to recall the journey made by the Prophet Muhammad S.A.W. from Makkah to Madinah in 622 CE. Muslims celebrate the establishment of their religious community and gifts may be exchanged.

POSSIBLE ACTIVITIES

- Recount the story of the hijran (meaning departure, exit or emigration). Show the children on a map where the journey took place and use a time line to give them a sense of how long ago it happened.
- Talk about how the beginning of a new year can be a time to recall important links within the community and family, and to focus on what really matters for the coming year.
- Explore with older children the existence of different calendar systems and year datings. Different faiths count from the most significant event for that religion. The Muslim year is 1420 in the Western year 1999, because the lunar year is shorter than the Western solar year.

ID–UL–FITR

This significant festival is one of the times when Muslim families reaffirm their faith. The festival is always within the ninth month of the Muslim calendar and the name of the month is Ramadan. In 1999 Id-ul-Fitr fell on the 19th January and in 2000 will be on the 8th January.

Ramadan is important because Muslims believe that it was during this month that the Prophet Muhammad S.A.W. first heard the revelatory messages from God. Muslims fast during the hours of daylight throughout this month and Id-ul-Fitr marks the end of Ramadan. The festival is celebrated with special prayers, with visits to friends and family and a celebration meal. New clothes are often bought and children also receive presents of money and sweets. Id-ul-Fitr is a celebration not only of the end to the long period of fasting but of a challenge successfully faced.

POSSIBLE ACTIVITIES

- Talk with the children about the festival and read a book about celebrating within the family. For example *A story at Id* from the *World Religions* series published by Heinemann.
- Talk about why Muslims fast during the daylight hours of Ramadan. If you have Muslim children in your group, they can share their own feelings, if they wish, about joining part of the fasting period. Muslims fast to encourage self-discipline and to remind themselves of what it feels like to be hungry. You can make some links to other faiths in which people fast or give up foods for specific religious festivals. Perhaps discuss how children feel when they have managed a difficult task and experience the satisfaction of knowing they have faced a challenge.

Making cards

- Make greetings cards. The patterns can be complex but must not feature any people or animals. According to the teachings of the Qur'an, it is blasphemous to depict living creatures. You can use a wide range of stylised flowers, star and moon shapes and abstract patterns.
- Buy some Id cards if some are available locally and make a display.

ID-UL-ADHA

Early years and school settings in areas with few if any Muslim families often only celebrate Id-ul-Fitr. However, for Muslims the celebration of Id-ul-Adha, the festival of sacrifice is at least as important, probably more so. Id-ul-Fitr is also called Id-ul-Saghir (the lesser Id) and British Muslim children may call it 'Little Id'. This name is in contrast with Id-ul-Adha, also known as Id-ul-Kabir (the greater Id) and you may hear children call it 'Big Id', a symbol of its importance to the Muslim community.

Id-ul-Adha is a four-day festival, within the final month of the Muslim calendar. (It falls within the Western calendar month of March in the year 2000.) Muslims at this time remember the willingness of the Prophet Ibrahim (Abraham of the Jewish Torah and Christian Old Testament) to sacrifice his son Isma'il for Allah, who intervened to stop the boy's death.

The festival also celebrates the completion of the annual pilgrimage to Makkah to visit the Mosque where the Prophet Muhammad S.A.W. is buried. The pilgrimage (the Hajj) is one of the obligations of Muslims (see page 29) and is itself a form of personal sacrifice. Id-ul-Adha is a time for Muslims to remember their shared identity and responsibilities as a community of worshippers established by the Prophet Muhammad S.A.W.

Families celebrate together and eat a special meal, of lamb or sheep, and a range of savoury and sweet dishes. Families may wear new clothes and there may be an exchange of gifts and cards. As at Id-ul-Fitr, the festival is also a time to give to those less fortunate in the community and part of the meat in the celebration meal is traditionally given to poorer families.

POSSIBLE ACTIVITIES

- Tell the story of Ibrahim and Isma'il. Like many important religious stories this account raises some difficult moral issues about obligation and conflicts of loyalty.
- Discuss ways in which the children might give to people less fortunate than themselves, or reflect on helpful projects that you have all undertaken over the year. Open up the discussion to include gifts of time and attention and not only tangible things like giving money to charity.
- Talk with children about pilgrimage, both the Muslim Hajj and the role of pilgrimage in other faiths. Muslims undertaking the Hajj wear a simple white garment that symbolises the equality of pilgrims and their willingness to forego the usual social trappings.

Hinduism

HOLI: FEBRUARY OR MARCH

Holi is a five-day spring festival full of colour and lively games, processions and bonfires. The event crosses the boundaries of caste in Hindu society (see page 40). Customs vary and include throwing popcorn onto the bonfires and eating roasted coconut. Sometimes children are carried around the bonfire in a ritual designed to protect them from harm. On the morning of the second day there is a lively tradition that people go out into the streets and hurl coloured powder or spray coloured water over friends and family.

Two legends are linked with the festival of Holi:

- The miraculous saving of **Prahlada** through his faith in Vishnu and Rama (one manifestation of Vishnu in human form). Prahlada's father was a great king who declared himself a god and demanded worship.

However, his young son remained true to Vishnu and saved himself from several attacks on his life by speaking the God's name. Then his aunt, **Holika**, took Prahlada into the fire with her, claiming that she alone would not be harmed. However, she died in the flames and it was Prahlada whose faith in Vishnu saved him. Holika is sometimes burned in effigy on the Holi bonfire.

- The story of how Krishna defeated the evil **Putana**. When Krishna was a baby his uncle **Kansa** ordered a massacre of all children in order to ensure the death of Krishna. Putana was a female demon who took on human form and went around the country sucking the life out of any children she found. The baby Krishna recognised Putana's real self and destroyed her by sucking her life's blood instead. There is some suggestion that Putana represents winter and that her death and cremation brings winter to an end so that spring can begin.

POSSIBLE ACTIVITIES

- There will be a terrible mess if you follow the tradition of throwing coloured paints or water over each other, however much the children might enjoy it. Alternatively you could make a large paper frieze of figures or life-size cut-outs of the children, prop it up in the garden and do some hurling from a distance.

- Tell one or both of the stories that are associated with the festival. Both tales are fairly bloodthirsty but, frankly, so are many stories underlying festivals and faith (not to mention legends and traditional fairy tales). You can recount a version that is not too heavy on incineration or gore. Try for instance, *The story of Prahlad* from the *Stories from World Religions* series published by Heinemann.

RAKSHA BANDHAN: JULY OR AUGUST

This is a festival celebrating protection and care between brothers and sisters or between close friends of opposite sexes. Raksha means protection and bandhan means to tie. The festival has its source in several stories:

- Krishna had two sisters, one of whom was adopted, and they were jealous of each other. One day Krishna had a bad cut on his hand and his birth sister went in search of a bandage. However his adopted sister tore a piece of material from her sari to protect the cut immediately and Krishna never forgot her unselfish action.

- When **Indra** and **Indrana** were fighting the demon **Bali**, Vishnu gave Indrana a thread to tie round her husband's wrist and this protected him.

- A slightly different story is told of the King and Queen of Rajasthan which was under attack from Gujarat. The Queen went to a neighbouring state and asked for help from the King of that state by tying a **rakhi** on his wrist and making him her honorary brother. This King helped to protect Rajasthan.

These stories are remembered in the festival when girls make or buy twisted white, red and gold thread bracelets (rakhi) which they give to their brothers or boys whom they regard as a brother. In their turn, the boys promise to protect their sister or friend.

The cultural focus of the festival is to recognise and strengthen the bond between brothers and sisters. Raksha Bandhan is a family festival when adult brothers and sisters will try hard to visit each other. In Hindu families the sister will mark her brother's forehead with red powder to form a **bindi**, tie on the prepared rakhi and offer him sweets like **barfi**. He in turn will promise her protection for the coming year and may have brought a gift or money.

ACTIVITIES

- Make a rakhi by twisting or plaiting thread, wool or other materials that the children can handle easily. Rakhi can be very simple or elaborate, with decorations such as beads, sequins and flower shapes. So children have a range of possibilities.
- Tell one or more of the stories that underlie the festival.
- Talk about the importance of support and protection amongst people who care for each other. Children may have examples of times when they were pleased to have loyalty and support from friends and family, as well as occasions when they were the ones who gave the protection. Conversations with children about brothers and sisters may bring out complaints about the unfairness of siblings, so be prepared.
- Buy some barfi if you can get it locally. Alternatively make something similar. Recipes vary for barfi but they involve boiling up ingredients which is unlikely to be possible for most readers. You can try an uncooked version by mixing 200g of desiccated coconut, 100g of icing sugar and a small tin of condensed milk. You could also add a few drops of food colouring. Form the mixture into small balls and add some nuts or cherries as decoration or roll in icing sugar. Let the sweets dry and put into small paper cases.

DIVALI: OCTOBER OR NOVEMBER

This five-day festival falls on a moonless night in the autumn and is also celebrated by Sikhs (see page 149). In Hinduism, the two main themes of Divali are:

- Reverence for the deva Lakshmi (also the wife of Vishnu), who is associated with wealth and good fortune and who is said to visit every Hindu home once a year. By the time Lakshmi visits, all family disagreements and any debts must be settled; the New Year then starts afresh.
- The story of Rama's rescue of Sita from the ten-headed demon king **Ravana**. Rama and Sita had been living in exile, forced out of the kingdom by Rama's scheming stepmother. Then Ravana kidnapped Sita using his trickery and Rama and his brother **Lakshman** set out to find and rescue Sita. Helped by **Hanuman**, the monkey king, they fought a great battle and defeated and killed Ravana. Then Rama and Sita travelled home to find that his father, the old King, had died. The city welcomed the return of Rama and Sita with many tiny lamps and he was crowned the rightful king. This story is only one part of the epic tale of the Ramayana.

The name Divali comes from the diwa or small lamps that are placed in the windows of Hindu homes to welcome Lakshmi. Divali celebrations usually include fireworks, the exchange of cards and gifts, including food. Oil lamps or candles are lit in the Mandir and homes are cleaned thoroughly. Tiled floors are scrubbed ready for the **Rangoli** pattern to be drawn, which welcomes Lakshmi into family homes. Coins are sometimes left for Lakshmi. Divali is a festival symbolising the triumph of light over darkness, knowledge over ignorance and good over evil.

Possible activities

- Talk about the festival and the idea of starting afresh in a New Year. Other festivals, including different change of year celebrations, also focus on resolving quarrels and making amends.
- Explore the story of Rama's rescue of his wife Sita. You could read this story from a book. Other possibilities are to tell the story with figures or puppets that the children help to make. Older children may enjoy creating a short play from the events.
- Tell the children how old this story is: it has been recounted for 4000 years. Explore with the children how a story can last for this long without being lost or forgotten. Make the link to the importance of oral traditions and story tellers.
- The Ramayana is an epic tale with many exciting parts, but is also a holy text for Hindus because of its spiritual messages (see page 36). Older children will be ready to discuss some of these ideas in a simple form and to appreciate the difficult decisions that Rama faced.

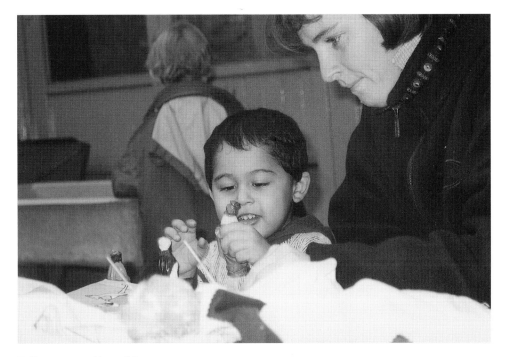

Telling a story with small figures

- Help children to make a version of the small diva lamps by using modelling or salt dough or clay. Start with a small ball and shape into a bowl shape by pressing a thumb into the middle and creating a container for a basic night light candle. The children can mark a pattern round the outside of the candle holder. You do not have to light the candles if you are very concerned about safety. However, a stable base to the candle holder and careful adult supervision should ensure safety for the children and allow them to experience the important symbol of real light.
- Make Divali cards. Possible illustrations can be of Lakshmi seated in a lotus flower, the shapes of the flower, the figures of Rama and Sita or diva lamps.
- Rangoli patterns are often drawn on the floor but you could draw one on a large sheet of paper or card. If you fill in areas with glue a few at a time, then children could decorate the pattern with sand, lentils or other material that will stick and create colour and texture. Smaller rangoli patterns could be coloured in or decorated. Rangoli patterns are built around a central point and the patterns are often flowers with four petals or squares divided in symmetrical triangles (four is a significant number in Hinduism). The pattern is repeated in a shape that can finally be round or square and the repetitive quality represents the endless cycle of time. An example is given opposite.

Example of a Rangoli pattern

- Make sweets like barfi or other foods that can be given. If you have a 'no sweets' policy in your setting you should perhaps consider relaxing the rules for special occasions such as Divali.
- Mendhi patterns are painted with henna on the hands of girls and women for a number of special occasions, for religious festivals and ceremonies like marriage. Henna is an effective dye so you would probably not paint children's hands. Some alternatives are to show children pictures of the complex hand decorations and try an activity of drawing round their hands and letting them create patterns on the cut-outs. This kind of hand painting is an Asian cultural custom and so you will also encounter it with Muslim families whose origins are Asian.

Buddhism

WESAK: MAY

This festival is the most important event in the Buddhist year because it is a threefold celebration of the birth, enlightenment and death of the Buddha. All these important events are believed to have occurred at the full moon during the same month (also called Wesak) of different years. Zen Buddhists celebrate only the birth of the Buddha at this time.

Buddhist celebrate Wesak by decorating homes and shrines with flowers, candles and lanterns. There are street processions and offerings of food and flowers to the Buddha at the Vihara. Buddhist monks receive gifts and special cards from children, who are given sweets in return.

POSSIBLE ACTIVITIES

- Read a book to the children, for example *The birth of the Buddha* from the *World Religions* series or *The Buddha's birthday* from *Bridges to Religions* series (both published by Heinemann).
- You could talk about the significance of the festival to Buddhist families, perhaps exploring the importance in beliefs of the birth of a very significant figure in any world faith.
- Although not associated only with Wesak, you could show the children examples of the detailed geometric mandalas that help Buddhists to focus and meditate. The mandalas would be complicated to make but children can appreciate a clear, coloured picture and perhaps trace the complexity with their fingers.
- Talk with children about the exchange of gifts in festivals and the reasons why giving and receiving is so important in families who celebrate within many world faiths.

KATHINA DAY: OCTOBER OR NOVEMBER

This festival marks the end of the rainy season in South East Asia and is a time when Buddhists give monks new robes in thanks for their spiritual guidance. Through the rainy season the monks remain in their monastery or other sheltered place and spend the time in contemplation.

POSSIBLE ACTIVITIES

- Discuss with children how the passing of the seasons affects the kind of life it is possible to lead. Explain the impact of the rainy season in countries that have a long period of regular and very heavy rain. The children will probably be able to understand the relief when a long period of any kind of hard weather comes to an end.
- Explore how it is possible to wear robes made of long lengths of cloth rather than the clothes with which children will be more familiar. They could experiment with ways of winding cloth about them so that it stays put and they can still move around.
- Look at some photographs of Buddhist monks and perhaps contrast them with the appearance and clothing of spiritual figures from other world faiths. Discuss with the children why the spiritual leaders of a faith may dress differently from the general population.

Yuan Tan – Chinese New Year: January or February

The background

In the second half of the twentieth century, China was dominated by the communist political system in which religious beliefs were far from welcome. However, Chinese culture has historically been influenced by Buddhism and also by Confucianism (a system of social ethics established about 2500 years ago) and Taoism (a philosophical system of an equally long tradition). Reverence for family ancestors has also remained an important part of life.

China is the source of the world's oldest lunar calendar and their years run on a 12-year cycle named after certain animals, which it is believed were the only creatures to answer the Buddha's call. In response, the Buddha offered each animal a year to take its name and express symbolically its character through the personality and behaviour of everyone born within the twelve month period. For instance, 1998-9 is the Year of the Tiger, 1999-2000 the Year of the Rabbit (the Hare or the Cat in some traditions), 2000-1 the Year of the Dragon, 2001-2 the Year of the Snake and 2002-3 the Year of the Horse. Chinese astrology is based on the year in which children are born, whereas the Western astrological system has twelve signs, each of which cover about a month within the calendar year.

The Chinese New Year is celebrated with fireworks, giving sweets, flowers and other gifts. A substantial lion costume is supported by a number of dancers and the lion dance goes on throughout the day to the sound of drums and cymbals. The dragon procession is also popular because dragons are a symbol of good fortune. Yuan Tan is special time for children, who receive a red packet containing money to bring good luck. The packets themselves (**lai see**) have messages of good fortune written on them.

The first full moon of the New Year is celebrated with **Teng Chieh**, the Lantern Festival which will fall sometime in February. Many lanterns are made in various designs and strung out as decorations to welcome the coming of longer days.

Possible activities

- You can talk about the celebration and read about what the New Year means to Chinese families and their children.
- Make a lion mask or a dragon. You could make a three-dimensional sculpture or else paper dragons make an effective wall frieze.

- Make lai see with children and talk about what kind of good fortune you could wish each other for the coming year. You might need to encourage the children to think about possible enjoyable events rather than tangible presents or special trips.
- You could make paper and card lanterns and hang them in your setting.
- There can be a natural link into talking about how the seasons revolve and helping children to become alert to the shift from longer days in the summer to darker evenings in the autumn and then around once more to lighter afternoons and evenings.

Sikhism

After much discussion the Sikh community worldwide has decided to fix the dates of most festivals. The dates for 1999 given below have been decided in Amritsar and are likely to remain as those days in future years. The exception is the birthday of Guru Nanak, but this festival may be fixed in the future.

THE BIRTHDAY OF GURU GOBIND SINGH: 5TH JANUARY

At this time the Sikh community recalls the birth and life of Guru Gobind Singh who established Sikhism in the form that it exists today and ended the human succession of Gurus.

POSSIBLE ACTIVITIES

- On the relevant day, recount the story of Guru Gobind Singh (see page 50).
- Talk with the children about how birthdays are often celebrated, not only of important spiritual leaders. Explore how a birthday can be a time to focus on an individual, not just about presents.

BAISAKHI: 14TH APRIL

The Baisakhi festival is important for several reasons:
- Both Sikhs and Hindus celebrate Baisakhi as the first day of the new year and in the Punjab the day is also important as the end of the spring harvest.
- Baisakhi is especially important to Sikhs as the day that Guru Nanak started his travels to spread the message of Sikhism beyond the Punjab.
- Guru Amar Das (the third Guru) established the tradition that Sikhs celebrate this day in order to create a distinct identity from other faiths.
- Then Guru Gobind Singh (the tenth Guru) chose the time of the festival for the formation of the Khalsa (see page 50) which set the important pattern of membership of and commitment to the Sikh community.

POSSIBLE ACTIVITIES

There are several layers to the Baisakhi festival and you do not want children to become confused.

- You could tell the story of Guru Nanak and the beginning of the Sikh faith (or save this story for the birthday of Guru Nanak).
- You can recount the events of the formation of the Khalsa and its significance for Sikhism. It is possible for the children to act out some of this exciting sequence of events. However, nobody should be Guru Gobind Singh, since this would be regarded as disrespectful by Sikhs.
- During Baisakhi the Guru Granth Sahib is read aloud in the gurdwara in periods of two hours by five men. Perhaps talk with the children about the importance of reading significant scriptures so that everyone can hear. How might they share out the reading of important material, perhaps in school assembly?
- When the reading is complete, new members are admitted into the Sikh community (see page 53). Perhaps talk with the children about how faiths and communities often have clothing or other visible signs to show belonging. What might be the reasons for this action?
- The local Sikh community will also celebrate with a communal meal in the langar, followed by singing and dancing. You could plan and organise with the children a simple snack or meal to which people are invited. Alternatively try some of the sweets (**karah parshad**) or savoury food (**dhal**, vegetable curry and **chappatis**) that is served at Baisakhi.

DIVALI: 5–7TH NOVEMBER

This festival falls in late autumn and is celebrated by Sikhs and Hindus (see page 142). At Divali Sikhs celebrate the release from Gwailor prison of Guru Har Gobind. The Sixth Guru refused to be released unless 52 Hindu princes were also given their freedom. The Mughal Emperor Jehangir agreed but demanded that only those princes could leave who were able to pass out of the narrow passage from the prison holding onto the clothes of Guru Har Gobind. He succeeded by wearing a cloak with very long tassels and so was able to leave safely with all 52 princes holding onto part of his cloak.

Divali celebrations include fireworks, the exchange of cards and gifts, including food. Oil lamps or candles are lit in the Gurdwara.

POSSIBLE ACTIVITIES

- Talk about the festival and that both Sikhs and Hindus celebrate at this time but for different reasons.

- Recount the story of Guru Har Gobind and his successful strategy to save the Hindu princes.
- With older children you could talk about the importance of religious tolerance in Sikhism and how Guru Har Gobind was willing to give up his own freedom rather than leave people behind in jail, who were of a different religion to himself.

THE BIRTHDAY OF GURU NANAK: OCTOBER

This important time recalls the birth of the founder of Sikhism, although according to some sources he was born in April. This festival celebrates the beginning of the faith, when the community remembers the original teachings of Guru Nanak.

POSSIBLE ACTIVITIES

- Recount the story of Guru Nanak and the start of the Sikh faith. The Heinemann series *Stories from World Religions* has a title on *Guru Nanak*.
- Make links to other important birthdays that you may have celebrated in connection with world faiths.

Common themes in the celebration of festivals

You will notice that the main festivals in world faiths share common themes, which reflect the concerns of people in many parts of the world and through history. With care, you can explore such shared themes and their importance to children and adults whilst keeping the faiths distinct and showing respect. Good practice in helping children to learn about different faiths can support them to find concerns in common with children and families who may initially seem very different. It is possible to help children to find communality with others and still show in simple terms that faiths are distinct. These possible themes are discussed in more detail below:

- Festivals of light
- The struggle to do what is right
- A fresh start
- Family life and children
- Food as part of celebrations
- Dressing for the occasion
- Giving to others
- Special journeys
- Oral traditions.

Festivals of light

- The theme of bringing light where there was darkness, darkness as a symbol of ignorance or fear, light as a source of guidance or lighting the way to safety.
- Some festivals of light, such as Divali, also have their cultural origins in hospitality to travellers.
- Use of candles as a symbol and as a source of actual light: Advent, Hannukah and Divali.

The struggle to do what is right

- Many festivals and associated stories highlight the struggle between good and evil as symbolised by individual people or the blend of good and bad in everyone. See also page 155 for a discussion of using stories.
- Stories such as the epic tale of Rama and Sita illustrate a human struggle between personal preferences, loyalty to loved ones and duty.
- Fasting or voluntary limitations to what is eaten are part of an exercise in discipline and a sense of satisfaction in managing to follow the code.

A fresh start

- The importance of a fresh start, a time to reflect on mistakes and to vow to improve, to resolve quarrels and start anew.
- Many festivals have the idea of renewal, symbolised by new clothes and cleaning homes.
- Some festivals encourage people to take stock and to contemplate their actions past and present. New Year festivals are sometimes seen as a time to plan for personal improvement.

Family life and children

- The significance of families and spending time together in celebration, giving thanks and remembering significant events within a shared past.
- Some festivals emphasise the importance of the broader community as everyone gets together in the streets or locality to celebrate.
- Valuing children through giving them a part to play in important celebrations as well as the giving of gifts. Helping children to learn about a shared history and heritage.
- Making the effort to be with one's family when you live some distance apart. Celebrations such as the Chinese New Year, Christmas or Raksha Bandhan are examples of times when relatives try to see each other and spend time together.

- Families and close friends supporting one another, offering loyalty and protection.

Food as part of celebrations

- Celebrating together, including a shared meal, which may have specific traditional foods.
- Some food may have special meaning within a festival and are in themselves symbols of events that the celebration recalls, for instance, the importance of each food in the traditional Pesach meal for Jewish families.
- Food to break a period of fast, for instance at Id–ul–Fitr or to celebrate the reintroduction of foods that have been avoided for a time, for instance breaking the Lent fast.
- Some festivals and ceremonies such as naming new babies involve foods that are a treat, such as different kinds of sweets or rich puddings.
- Giving thanks for food is also part sometimes of the celebration.

Dressing for the occasion

- Some festivals stress the importance of new or a clean set of clothes as part of a sense of renewal.
- Other celebrations encourage people to dress up in fancy clothes, hats or masks that are not usually worn. Some outfits will have special meaning for the festival.

Giving to others

- The exchange of gifts, including food and sweets traditional to the festival.
- Hospitality and sharing food with others. Inviting others to join you in celebration or meals.
- Awareness of others less fortunate than oneself, giving gifts or time to others.

Special journeys

- The significance of pilgrimage, either remembering an important journey made by spiritual leaders or the attempt by followers to take a similar or identical pilgrimage.
- Children can gain an understanding of special journeys that have meaning to the travellers or that are undertaken to revive important beliefs or shared memories. Religious pilgrimages are a particular kind of journey in that part of the experience is often that pilgrims should leave behind luxuries or visible signs that disrupt a sense of equality between believers.

- Making the effort to visit family and friends at a time of celebration, even if they live at some distance.

Oral traditions

- The importance of oral traditions is reflected in many faiths and the patterns followed within celebrations. Some of the holy scriptures, for instance the Qur'an, were originally held in the memory of followers before being written down to avoid the risks of unauthorised or unintended changes. Memorising sections of holy scriptures is a significant part of religious practice in many faiths. Stories and question-and-answer sequences are another way that children are taught about important ideas and events, for instance during Pesach for Jewish families.
- Celebrations can be a time to explore the age of some of the important stories told and retold in world faiths: the Ramayana is 4000 years old, stories of Jesus from the New Testament are about 2000 years old, stories told in Jewish festivals are 2-3000 years old. Children might explore what makes a good story last, why people keep retelling them and the messages that they communicate.

Further resources

A range of books are available that will help you to support children's understanding of different celebrations. All the books are well illustrated and attractive for children to look at before they are ready to read the text for themselves. Young children like browsing through good reference books and their interest will support their growing literacy skills. Many of the suggestions for children will also provide ideas and information for you.

BOOKS FOR CHILDREN

- The *Celebrations* series published by A & C Black has photographs and simple text suitable for younger children and early primary school. Titles include *Dat's New Year, Diwali, Eid-ul-Fitr, New Baby, Sam's Passover* and *Wedding*. (The spelling is as used in the books.)
- *Festivals through the Year* includes four titles written by Anita Ganeri which organise celebrations from many faiths and cultures by the four seasons (published by Heinemann).
- *Celebrate* is a series of six books written by different authors and covering festivals of the six main faiths (published by Heinemann). The books are aimed at seven- to eleven-year-olds but good illustrations and the focus on children's experience make the series a possible resource for using with slightly younger children.

- The *World of Festivals* series is written by different authors and published by Evans. The books are illustrated and aimed at seven- to eleven-year-olds. Current titles include *Chinese New Year, Christmas, Passover, Holi, Ramadan and Id-ul-Fitr, All Saints, All Souls and Halloween, Easter, Carnival, Divali, Hanukkah* and *Thanksgiving and other Harvest Festivals.*
- The four books in the *Festivals of the World* series published by Heinemann focuses on countries: Mexico, Germany, India and Israel. Both religious and cultural festivals are covered and there are some suggestions for craft and food activities. The books are aimed at older primary school children.
- The Franklin Watts *Fiesta* series also organises the titles by country. Aimed at seven- to eleven-year-olds the books cover a wide range of festivals, explaining the traditions underlying events, relevant stories and possible activities that you can undertake with children. Currently the titles cover Brazil, China, Germany, India, Ireland, Israel, Italy, Jamaica, Japan, Korea, Mexico, Nigeria, Peru, Russia, Turkey and Vietnam.
- The 'Children just like me' series (Dorling Kindersley) includes *Celebration* by Barnabas and Anabel Kindersley which covers a range of festivals.

RESOURCES FOR ADULTS

- Fitzjohn, Sue, Weston, Minda and Large, Judy (1993) *Festivals together – a guide to multi-cultural education* (Hawthorn Press).
- *Shap Calendar of Religious Festivals*, a booklet and calendar which is updated regularly and a book, *Festivals in World Religions*, both available from The Shap Working Party (address on page 181).
- The weekly magazine *Nursery World* has regular seasonal features on festivals from different faiths. *Child Education* also has some features with ideas suitable for primary school age children. *Coordinate* (from the National Early Years Network) sometimes has relevant articles to help you to think about the issues.
- You will also find material about religious and cultural celebrations in some of the books suggested on page 56.

8

Supporting children's learning

Introduction

This chapter covers a number of ways of extending children's learning about faiths and human concerns. The different sections of the chapter are not mutually exclusive, but rather describe some possible approaches to learning. These include:

- Using books and stories
- Taking children on visits
- Learning about religious artefacts
- Broad learning from religious education
- Applications of faith to everyday living.

Using books and story-telling

This section contains details of resources and suggestions on how to use them.

Reading and telling stories

Faiths can come alive for children through the medium of stories. There is a wide choice of books that recount important events in the life of spiritual leaders and significant moral tales from different faiths. It will be appropriate to read some stories at the time of the relevant celebration but others are potentially suitable at any time of the year. I have made a number of suggestions for books from page 157, although obviously you will need to make a final choice depending on the age and understanding of the children with whom you work. There are also many tales of spiritual and human significance in the area of myths and legends and these are discussed from page 158.

The main stories from all the world faiths tend to have several layers to the telling:

- Many stories are exciting and seize the attention of listeners in their own right.

- All carry some message for the audience, either about a faith, key beliefs or how a faith became established.
- Often stories also raise moral issues and difficult decisions in a natural way through the events of the tale.

Effective practice in using stories with children depends on some sensible approaches, taking account of children's age and understanding. Additionally, adults should never forget that most children have a sharp sense of when they are being pushed towards a moral point with no discussion permitted.

- The main point about any story is that it has to interest children and be read aloud in a way that engages and holds children's attention. Choose well-written books with good illustrations and the right amount of text for this group.
- Once they have become interested, children will want to know what happens and ask for good stories many times.
- Longer stories can be read a bit each day in episodes, which involves the children in recalling 'where we finished last time…'
- Older children will start to read some stories to themselves.
- Consider telling some stories, either without any props or perhaps with some pictures on a magnetic or other board. When children know stories well they want to join in the telling.
- Shared story telling can easily move across to using small models of the characters or puppets, or to the development of small dramatic role plays, if the children want.

Even young children often have something to say about a tale. They may have questions along the lines of 'Why did she do that . . .?' or 'What did he think he was doing when …?' They may also have questions of fact such as, 'Did this really happen?' or 'Did she or he really look like the pictures?'

- Older children can be motivated to discuss characters, events, feelings and the choices that arose in a story when the best decision is far from clear.
- Opportunities for further exploration may arise after the telling of a story, through circle time or individual conversation.

It is difficult to predict how a certain story will catch children's attention and which issues they will most want to discuss. Certainly, children's attention will be lost if adults insist on pursuing the moral of the tale as they see it. Some faith stories raise serious moral issues, for instance 'the promised land', to which the Israelites travelled claiming it as their own (Judaism and also recounted in the Christian Old Testament stories), was already inhabited by other people with a different culture and religion. The parables told by Jesus Christ and recounted in the New Testament often raise moral questions to which there is no simple answer.

Some background information is often useful for children to understand a story in its time and place. For instance, Jesus' parable of the Good Samaritan, who went out of his way to help a stranger who had been attacked, would have carried an extra edge at the time since his Jewish listeners did not like Samaritans. Additionally the details of the story were very challenging to the audience since one of the people who ignored the stranger was a Jewish priest.

SUGGESTIONS FOR FAITH STORIES

You need a good choice of books that recount the main stories from world religions in a way suitable for children. Some possibilities include:

- The *Stories from world religions* series by W. Owen Cole and Judith Lowndes is published by Heinemann. This series has 12 titles covering stories drawn from the six main faiths. Each story is told through simple text suitable for reading aloud to young children or for primary school children who can read to themselves.
- *Stories from the Bible* retold by Marcia Williams and published by Heinemann includes books for young children about Noah, Jonah and Joseph.
- The *Bible Stories* series from Heinemann is aimed at primary school age children and includes five retold stories from the Old and New Testament.
- Annabel Shilson-Thomas has written two books for Puffin: *A first Puffin Picture Book of Stories from World Religions* and *A First Puffin Picture Book of Bible Stories*. The approach is suitable for nursery and early primary school age children. The stories are told simply and the books include some commentary that will support your explanations.
- Dorling Kindersley publish the *Family Bible* (1997) and the *Children's Bible* (1994). Both of these books are well illustrated and accessible in layout. The *Family Bible* has the text of the Old and New Testaments in ordinary English and is suitable for use with older children. The *Children's Bible* has the bible stories retold by Selena Hastings in a way suitable for primary school children. The layout makes it easy to read the stories and to discuss moral issues that arise from events.
- The *Tales of Heaven and Earth* series from Moonlight Publishing (distributed by Ragged Bears, tel: 01264 772269) includes 13 titles taken

from a range of world faiths. Children would need to be competent readers to use these books alone (the series is aimed at Key Stages 3 and 4) but the well told stories are ideal for reading aloud in episodes to primary school children. The titles have high quality illustrations and short explanatory points next to the text that will help you to answer questions from children or your own queries. A few examples from the series are *Muhammed's Night Journey* (Islam), *When Brendan Discovered Ireland* (Christianity), *Rama the Heroic Prince* (Hinduism), *The Prince who became a Beggar* (Buddhism) and *I'll tell you a story* (Judaism).

- *Stories from the Bible*, also from Moonlight Publishing, includes tales from the Old Testament, titles currently include the stories of Joseph, Noah and Moses.
- *Stories from the Christian World* retold by David Self and *Stories from the Jewish World* retold by Sybil Sheridan are both published by Macdonald Young Books. The books could be read aloud to three- to five-year-olds and enjoyed by young readers in the primary school.
- Ranchor Prime retold the story of Rama and Sita in *Ramayana: a journey* (Channel Four Books, 1997). The story is supported with illustrations and boxed explanations that would support your reading. The book is suitable for older children and to be read to them in episodes.
- Adiccabandhu and Padmasri recount the story of *Siddharta and the swan*, (Windhorse Publications, 1998).

THE VALUE OF MYTHS AND LEGENDS

Another source of thought-provoking stories can be found in the various series of myths and legends. Some of the stories in the suggested books are drawn from main world faiths but the remit is usually wider and includes less well known faiths and cultures around the world. Children are often inspired by tales of strength and weakness, good versus bad and unlikely or reluctant heroes and heroines. These books offer an engaging alternative to sanitised Disney characters and television cartoon superheroes, some of whom are rather one-dimensional, although not all. Many legends raise moral issues and tough questions that children may be interested to explore. Myths from a range of cultures around the world are also a valuable reminder that people from very different backgrounds wrestle with similar problems. Some possibilities include:

- Heinemann's *Myths and Legends* series which is written for seven- to eleven-year-olds and has 12 titles drawn from a range of different cultures.
- *Out of the Ark* and *Journeys Through Dreamtime* are both written by Anita Ganeri and published by Macdonald Young Books. The retold and

illustrated stories are drawn from a wide range of faiths.

- Sandy Shepherd retells 50 tales from around the world in *Myths and Legends*, published by Evans.
- Another possibility is *The Kingfisher Book of Mythology: gods, goddesses and heroes from around the world* (the stories are retold by many writers, published by Kingfisher Publications, 1998).
- Franklin Watts have three useful series all of which are aimed at seven- to eleven-year-olds and early secondary school students. *Landscapes of Legend* include six titles in the series which follows the theme of the natural phenomena which have inspired myths and fables. Different authors have written titles including *Sacred Skies*, *Mighty Mountains* and *Cities of Splendour*.
- *The Best Tales Ever Told* series has five titles so far and organises the tales by general themes of time and place, for instance, *Gods and giants: myths and legends of the Vikings, Celts and Middle Ages* and *Spirits and Sorcerers: myths and legends from Africa and Arabia*. The *Myths and Legends* series has a range of titles, some of which focus on myths of ancient Greece, some follow a broad theme, like *Creation Stories* or focus on one figure like *King Arthur*.

ACTIVITY

Read some of the suggested books before you read them to the children. Make sure that you look at titles from a range of cultures.

1. What themes can you see in common between different stories? What seems to concern humankind and how do myths and legends address people's anxieties and needs? You could look back at the discussion on page 1 about human needs, questions and the pressing desire to find answers, protection and some predictability in life.
2. Bear in mind that many of these myths and important stories were passed on for centuries through word of mouth rather than books. What makes a good story last?
3. Consider the importance in many cultures of experienced story-tellers. Make some local inquiries and see if you can invite a story-teller to visit your setting.

Reference books for children

You also need some books that bridge the gap between the sacred stories of different religions and what a faith means for a child and family day by day. There is now a wide choice of well-illustrated and informative books that bring faith alive in a way to which children can relate. The following series are suitable for children at the pre-school or primary school age. Some have simpler text but, because of the illustrations and attractive layout, all are suitable for interested children to look at as reference books. It is well worth remembering that many children enjoy browsing through non-fiction books before they are able to read the text. The following suggestions are all series with a range of titles:

- The *Bridges to Religion* series from Heinemann has five titles that approach aspects of faith through the experience of children and their families. Current titles include *An Egg for Babcha* (Catholic Christian) *Lucy's Sunday* (Anglican Christian), *The Seventh Day is Shabbat* (Judaism), *Something to Share* (Muslim) and *The Buddha's Birthday* (Buddhism).
- *Introducing religions* series written by Sue Penney for seven- to eleven-year-olds (published by Heinemann). Illustrated and highlighted text presents the six main faiths in six titles.
- The *Life Times* series written by Anita Ganeri and published by Evans. The series is aimed at seven- to eleven-year-olds but the high quality photographs and illustrations make the titles accessible to interested younger browsers. The major faiths are represented through four titles that focus on significant life events: *New Beginnings: celebrating birth, Growing up: from child to adult, Wedding Days: celebrations of marriage* and *Journey's End: death and mourning.*
- The *Holy Cities* series from Evans is aimed at seven- to eleven-year-olds and approaches faiths through significant holy places. Written by different authors, the titles include *Kyoto* (Buddhism and Shintoism), *Lhasa* (Buddhism), *Amritsar* (Sikhism), *Rome* (Catholic Christianity), *Jerusalem* (Christianity, Judaism and Islam) and *Mecca* (Islam).
- Franklin Watts publish three useful series. *Our Culture* has the simplest text with large photographs, aimed at five- to seven-year-olds and currently with six titles: *Buddhist, Hindu, Muslim, Jewish, Rastafarian* and *Sikh. Beliefs and Cultures* is aimed at seven- to eleven-year-olds and six titles cover the six main world faiths. Straightforward text is supported with good illustrations and suggested activities where appropriate. *My Belief* is aimed at seven- to eleven-year-olds and early secondary school students. The titles are well illustrated and take the personal approach of *I am a . . .,* including Anglican, Greek Orthodox, Roman Catholic and Pentecostal Christianity, Buddhist, Hindu, Jew, Muslim, Rastafarian and Sikh.

Taking children on visits

With some preparation, children can learn from visits to local places of worship, especially at times of the year that are especially significant for a particular faith. If you work in an area with a diverse population, you will have a choice of possible visits. However, do not assume that children will necessarily attend the places of worship in your community. For instance, families in a mainly white area are not necessarily active Christians and the main beliefs and worship may be unknown to children. Depending on your local area, it may be possible to arrange a visit to the local Church or Chapel (Christian), Vihara (Buddhist), Mandir (Hindu), Synagogue (Jewish), Mosque (Muslim) or Gurdwara (Sikh). If your area has very little diversity in faith, then you will need to extend the children's understanding through non-direct visual means, such as books, photo packs, illustrated wall friezes and videos. The organisations suggested from page 180 will useful to you and some books are suggested on page 162.

Planning for the visit

Children will learn more from their visit if it can be built into other activities that you are doing, although it does not have to be a large programme, especially for younger children.

WHAT QUESTIONS?

Discuss with children the kind of questions they might like to ask the religious leader. You could provide some written questions beforehand to the individual leader, as well as explaining what you would like the children to learn through their visit. Religious leaders are as variable as anyone else and some are better with groups of children than others. An individual who is at ease will soon show that she or he can happily deal with spontaneous questions when the children make the actual visit.

WHAT WOULD YOU LIKE TO EXPERIENCE?

Plan ahead for what you want the children to notice, for example:

- The shape and decoration of the outside of the building, as well as the inside. Some places of worship are highly decorated and some are more austere, or with a strong emphasis on simplicity.
- A useful visit is not all busy activity. Allow for time to encourage the children just to stand and look. Most places of worship have a special atmosphere, perhaps a sense of peacefulness. Let the children stand and feel the quiet or a sense of focus. They may grasp the reasons that some

people come to this place to pray, meditate or just sit in peace when there is no service in progress.

- Special displays appropriate to a current religious festival.
- The layout of the place, different areas of the building and what they mean.
- The symbols appropriate to this faith: where are they, what form do they take, how many examples can the children find?

Younger children may just look at the place of worship but primary school pupils will benefit from a worksheet or planner to help them gain from the visit. A class of children could be split into sub-groups who will explore different aspects. In this case, make sure that you allow some time the same day back in the classroom for the different groups to share a little of what they have learned.

A general discussion may also be appropriate. Bear in mind that many visits will happen when the place of worship is otherwise empty. So you may need to alert children to what happens when people gather in the building that they have had to themselves. Explore the reasons that people meet together regularly to worship within a faith and in a specially designed building. Some of the prepared questions that you give to the religious leader could well be about what happens during key services or ceremonies in this faith.

USING REFERENCE BOOKS

You need to ensure that you read around the topic for your own information. However, there are a good range of books that are suitable for children. The illustrations and text may be the only way to extend children's understanding when no such place of worship is within easy visiting distance. Some possibilities include:

- A & C Black publish a Keystones series in which titles are written through the eyes of children exploring different places of worship. The series includes *Buddhist Vihara*, *Christian Church*, *Hindu Mandir*, *Jewish Synagogue*, *Muslim Mosque* and *Sikh Gurdwara*.
- The *Places of worship* series from Heinemann focuses more on the buildings and aims to answer the kind of questions asked by primary school children. The series currently has four titles: *Synagogues*, *Protestant Churches*, *Mosques* and *Hindu Temples*.

Respectful behaviour on visits

Find out about appropriate behaviour for this place of worship before you go and do not make the visit unless you, and the children, will follow the normal rules for visitors or the congregation. If you have the option, talk with parents who attend your setting and know this place of worship. You can then follow up that conversation by contacting the relevant person within the faith (Vicar, Imam, Rabbi and so on).

•••••••••••••••••••• *Ideas for good practice* ••••••••••••••••••

- Shortly before the visit, talk through with the children what will be expected of them, for instance, peaceful behaviour rather than total silence. Express your requests positively in terms of courtesy and respect for any place of worship. If you give children a long list of 'don't's, they will anticipate a miserable outing and will not be in a good frame of mind to learn.

- Warn children and their parents in advance about any requirements for dress. For instance, some places of worship will ask that women and girls, and possibly also males cover their head. Many places of worship will request modest clothing for males and females, at least clothes that cover the upper legs and shoulders. This request may not be an issue in winter, but summer clothing may need some forethought. Some places of worship may be less concerned about what the children wear than the adult workers.

- Be ready to remove your shoes before entering the Vihara, Mandir, Gurdwara or Mosque. If children are not of these faiths, then explain in advance that removal is a gesture of respect. In the same way explain to children, for whom removal of footwear in a place of worship is normal behaviour, that not all faiths take this approach.

You could discuss with the children before and after the visit how there are many ways that members of the different faiths show respect. For instance, in Christian Churches, it is usually seen as a gesture of respect that men remove their hat, if they are wearing one. Yet women either are not required to remove a hat or may definitely be expected to cover their hair in some way.

RELIGIOUS SERVICES

Children will learn from visits to a few different places of worship. However, it is unlikely to be appropriate for you to take them to religious services, since that is the role of parents – as is any specific religious instruction in a given faith. The situation will be different in church schools since denominational collective worship is allowed and attendance at some religious services for the denomination or faith is more likely to be part of school life.

Learning about religious artefacts

Children can learn through good quality illustrations in books and photo packs. However, primary school children are also ready to appreciate some religious artefacts appropriate to the faith that they are exploring in RE.

A range of example artefacts and your explanations can help children to appreciate the different uses of certain items. For instance:

- Some items are respected in their own right, such as the different holy books from world faiths.
- Other items, such the rosary used by Catholic Christians, icons in the Orthodox church or mandalas in Hinduism or Buddhism are used to focus attention and help avoid distraction from prayer or meditation.
- Some religious artefacts are most important for their personal significance or providing comfort and inspiration. Visiting adults, or some team members, may be pleased to share such artefacts. A prayer book may be especially important because it was a gift at this person's confirmation (Christianity). This particular Seder plate (used in Jewish families to celebrate Pesach) may be particularly valued because it has passed down many generations of the family. A holy picture carried in a wallet or handbag may look very battered but is a prized possession because of the associations.

It is crucial that any artefacts or any activities with religious meaning are treated with respect and care. If you take a respectful approach then children are very likely to follow your good example. For instance, children should never pretend to pray, nor do joke meditation or obeisance. Your aim is to promote respect, not reverence. Children who attend places of worship with their families may show reverence within that context, but it is not your role to promote reverence in the pre-school or school setting.

• • • • • • • • • • • • • • • • • • *Ideas for good practice* • • • • • • • • • • • • • • • • • • •

Help the children to reflect and appreciate the artefacts. Ideally children should be able to touch as well as look at the artefacts:

- They will understand, if you explain, that precious personal

artefacts must be treated with great care. They can probably make the links to how they feel if something that matters to them is poorly handled.

- You will help children then to understand appropriate behaviour if you make a display of artefacts (not the personal items) rather than laying items out as if they were play materials.

- Sometimes you will explain immediately the nature of an artefact. However, on other occasions it may be suitable to encourage children to explore possible meanings on the basis of what they have already learned. Avoid a lengthy guessing game that risks becoming disrespectful or tedious.

- Help children to appreciate the details of an artefact: the complex pattern or striking simplicity, the bright colours of a new or the worn away quality of a much-used artefact.

Further resources

You will also have much to learn about faiths unfamiliar to you. Useful resources include:

- Thompson, Jan and Gateshill, Paul, *Religious Artefacts in the Classroom*, Hodder and Stoughton. The book provides ideas for appropriate and sensitive use of artefacts and there is an illustrated catalogue of the artefacts relevant to the six main world faiths.
- Weddell, Kathy, *Making the most of your artefacts*, a booklet from the Westhill RE Centre, address on page 122.
- The suppliers listed from page 180 are a good source of artefacts, especially if you have limited options to buy locally.

Broad learning from RE

The range of activities described in this chapter, and the celebrations described in Chapter 7, should be valued in their own right. Neither visits to places of worship nor religious and cultural celebrations should be reduced to handy resources in an early years or National Curriculum. For instance, Id-ul-Fitr does not exist in order to improve children's pen handling skills as they make a card. A visit to the local Mosque should not be absorbed so much into the current art project that the children do not grasp the religious significance of the building. You need to keep an open and flexible mind and then appropriate broad learning for children is a real possibility. Some examples follow.

Language and communication

Children have opportunities to learn when they:

- Are given the chance to express their views and to share information like 'what we do in my home . . .'. Such exchanges may happen in individual conversations or group conversation such as circle time.

- Listen to stories and comment on the characters and issues raised by important tales. Children may be able to discuss the problems of being torn between two obligations or when it is not hard to do what you feel is the right thing.
- Create and take part in simple dramatic reconstructions of some events or do puppet plays. They may present their work or a short drama to other children in the group, in school assembly or to parents in a special event.
- Make and illustrate their own books based on events and stories.
- Follow recipes for cooking special celebration foods.
- Improve their pencil control by drawing and colouring some of the complex designs.
- Extend their reading and writing work through any of the projects. Children can also become aware that languages around the world have different alphabets and direction of handwriting. Some children in the group may already be aware because of their home languages.

Social, personal and moral development

With careful adult attention and thought, there are opportunities to support children in the following ways:

- To extend children's understanding of the variety in human values, beliefs and activities and to give them a sense of the diversity in their own local community and further afield.
- Children can feel affirmed in their own identity so long as any work about faith extends to give respect to all families, including those who do not follow mainstream religions.
- You can build the basis for respect for beliefs and practices that children's families do not share, so long as you create a framework for learning that promotes genuine respect.
- Children can work together on activities linked with celebrations or visits, or in some of the traditional festival games.
- There can be chances to explore the importance of family life and friendship networks, for instance, in celebrations from many world faiths. This exploration can allow properly for the different kinds of families represented in the group.
- Many of the important stories in world faiths and the range of myths and legends raise significant moral issues that can be discussed with children in simple language. Difficult choices are faced by key religious figures or characters in important stories. Story events often illustrate that the

difference between right and wrong is not always straightforward and it is sometimes not at all easy to take what appears to be the right course of action.

- All the above ideas are important but you should never lose sight of even less tangible gains for children. Perhaps their most enduring memory of a celebration or a visit is of the beauty of what they have seen, the pleasure in watching a line of flickering candles or the amazing intricacy of a design or decoration.

Mathematics

There will be regular opportunities for children to use their mathematical skills as you help them to:

- Plan ahead for special activities: has the group got enough card and other materials, or how much food and drink will be needed for a special celebration meal?
- Counting, measuring and weighing will sometimes be important skills in cooking and craft activities. Some measurements, such as of a place of worship that is visited, may be important if you are planning to build a scale model when you get back.
- Shop for ingredients or to buy special foods for festivals. Children can handle the money and may be able to make some estimates of the final bill at the checkout.
- Understand different shapes and patterns and appreciate the intricacy of complex designs.
- Extend children's understanding of the passing of time. They can make and consult a year's calendar in which you mark the festivals that you will celebrate together this year (they need not be the same ones each year). You can use a time line of days to help the group to follow the passing of time relevant to specific festivals or times important to a faith. Possibilities include: the days from Shrove Tuesday through Lent and to Easter Sunday, the four weeks of Advent up to Christmas or the days passing in the month of fasting during Ramadan.

Science and the world around children

Basic science can arise when children:

- Explore changes during cooking celebration foods, because cooking can be seen as a kind of basic chemistry.
- Learn about the patterns of the year through different festivals linked to the seasons. They can also gain an insight into why seasonal changes can

matter so much and into the sources of their food, for instance through harvest festivals.

- Grow flowers from seeds or bulbs, perhaps for Easter or experiment with growing their own vegetables in time for a small harvest festival in the autumn.
- Explore different kinds of material and what they can do, perhaps through the arts and crafts activities.
- Explore in a simple way the differences between a lunar and solar calendar. Children could make observations of the passing phases of the moon during the time of year when the onset of darkness is in the late afternoon or early evening. Urban children will not have as clear a view of the night sky as children in small towns or a rural area, but some observations should be possible. You will need to enlist the parents' help on this kind of project.

Children can learn a great deal about the world around them through the kind of activities covered here. However, adults need to consider carefully the balance between information or explanation and enjoyment of a natural phenomenon. If children are to experience enchantment and the delight of curiosity, of sometimes not knowing, then adults have to resist the temptation either to push children to discover information or to share it. Enjoyable events are not always helped by being reduced to rational explanations.

· *To think about* ·

Do you dig up the rabbit?
Many early years and school settings have a pet, such as a rabbit, guinea pig or hamster. In the natural order of life, these pets will die. This occasion may be a suitable time to talk with children about sadness and the passing of someone for whom they care. It can also be appropriate to have a small ceremony to bury the pet, perhaps in the nursery or school garden.

Now, suppose that some of the children later express interest in what has happened to the dead animal. The spirit of pure scientific inquiry would suggest that you take the opportunity to dig up the pet and study decay at first hand. Susan Issacs, in her account of the Malting House School at Cambridge during the 1930s, gives just such an account of how the children were allowed to dig up the rabbit. On the other hand, an emotional or spiritual focus would suggest that the dead pet should be left in peace.

1. Think through a suitable explanation to children for each of the pos-

sible choices: the scientific investigation and the spiritual preference.
2. What do you think is the better approach and what are your reasons?
3. Discuss the example with your colleagues or fellow-students.

(Thank you to Helen McAuley for the conversation that led to this box. Incidentally, neither Helen nor I would dig up the rabbit.)

Art and music

Celebrations, visits and the resource of books and posters can effectively support children's opportunities to:

- Engage in a very wide variety of arts and crafts, with scope for choosing their own materials or patterns and extending their current level of skill. They can also experience the satisfaction of having made something themselves.
- Experiment with pattern, shape, colour and texture.
- Appreciate different art forms through books and posters and different cultural and religious traditions in artistic representation.
- Enjoy listening to and tuning into different kinds of music: singing, festival and dance music.

Technology and design

Many of art activities link with design and some further ideas include:

- Helping children to learn how to plan and design, as well as participate in a wide variety of arts and crafts.
- Enjoy and appreciate technically difficult designs.
- There might be a focus on making costumes, puppets, small figures and appropriate artefacts.
- Approaching shape and different design systems through the layout of places of worship.
- Sometimes children might be able to build a model of a place of worship that they have visited.

History

Children are ready to extend their understanding of time as they explore:

- When some events took place within the time span of known history. They can develop a basic sense of chronology and the idea of a time line.

- Opportunities for local history through faiths and the establishment of local religious and cultural celebrations.
- The time line of the arrival of some of the ethnic groups in a diverse community.
- Different sources of information on the same event: how do different versions develop and how do you weigh up accuracy.
- A combination of historical and geographical interests can be met in tracing how the different aspects of a celebration, such as Christmas, have developed.

Geography

Like History, children tend first to understand geography by working from what they can experience on a local basis. They can explore:

- The location of places of worship in the local neighbourhood and how, for some families, life in the community may revolve around faith and related activities. Urban children may have access to a range of places of worship, whereas children in rural areas may only have one or two.
- The location of some festivals held in Britain and around the world, which children are not likely to experience locally. Children can learn how to use a globe and a map.
- The idea of constant direction in terms of the compass points of north, south, east and west. This exploration could emerge from a discussion about the requirement that Muslims always face towards Makkah when they pray five times a day. When travelling, Muslims carry a compass in order to position themselves.
- Where in the world certain historical events took place that are recounted during some religious and cultural celebrations.
- Ways of mapping how the main world faiths spread out from their point of origin. For instance, Islam started in the Middle East and then spread to East Asia, India, Pakistan and into parts of Europe.
- Movements of people across countries, including the countries of origin of the many different ethnic groups now represented in the UK.

Applications of faith to everyday living

Personal care

Children learn about and are involved in approaches to diet, clothing, and hygiene that are integral to the family faith. It is important that children can follow these guidelines without embarrassment or being made to feel odd within a group. Attention to the details of personal care is important for your practice with children because your behaviour can show respect in action and support children's sense of personal identity derived from their family faith or philosophical position. This approach is a requirement arising from the Children Act 1989 (see page 107) but should be part of a courteous and respectful approach to children whether or not your setting comes under this legislation.

Food and drink

It should be normal practice that staff in an early years, playwork or school setting ask parents about what their children eat, or do not eat. Some children have allergies to certain foodstuffs and these must be avoided. Some families will request that their children are not given particular food or drink because these are unacceptable for religious reasons. Some families may also follow a particular diet, perhaps be vegetarian, for philosophical reasons. Some requests should be respected and followed. If there is a genuine difficulty in meeting a request then this should be discussed with parents. A way to resolve the situation needs to be found that does not leave parents believing wrongly that their request has been met. Nor should children be placed in an impossible position, because they either have to eat food they know is not right for their family or go hungry.

Any requests about food and drink, like any issues about care, need to be communicated to all the staff who will have contact with children. Good patterns of communication can be especially important in schools where teachers or nursery nurses may have the conversation with parents, but other support staff supervise the children at mealtimes.

Without doubt, within a diverse population area, settings can face a wide range of requests about food. There will be limits to how many variations can be offered within a budget and available kitchen facilities. One very practical approach is to ensure that children always have a proper and attractive vegetarian option for every mealtime. This meal will meet the needs of a range of children who, for different reasons, may wish to avoid the alternatives of meat or poultry. For any children, or colleagues, who are vegetarian, you need to get into the habit of checking the ingredients of processed and convenience foods. Some products surprisingly include meat-derived ingredients, such as gelatine or rennet. (There are vegetarian alternatives for both.) Some cheap ice creams also include animal fat.

BE AWARE OF ATTITUDES

Food preferences and traditions vary considerably but unaware workers in any setting may take the approach that their own familiar tradition is the 'normal way' of eating and any variation must therefore be 'odd' or 'faddy'. This view is unacceptable because such workers are showing very narrow ways of thinking and such attitudes will seep into a disrespectful way of behaving towards children or parents. Of course, what you know best in any area of life, especially from your own childhood, will initially seem like the ordinary way. However, within care, playwork and education settings you have a responsibility to think beyond what is familiar to you. Part of your role with children is to extend their experience and you need to be open to learning yourself as well.

ACTIVITY

You will hear some people claim that they 'eat anything' or you may read booklets that describe food preferences based on religious reasons as following a 'restricted diet'. Both statements are misleading. For instance, British people who happily eat meat are not usually willing to eat every edible animal, bird or fish, even those happily eaten in other parts of the world. Closer to home, some mainland European countries regard the British habit of eating lamb with just as much resistance as most British people show about eating horse meat.

Think about and note down the foods that you:

1. Are pleased to eat on a regular basis.
2. Would prefer not to eat, but could manage in order to be polite or to avoid going hungry.
3. Could not face eating under any circumstances.

Look over your list and ideally discuss it with a colleague or fellow-student. For instance, are you now aware that some food that you like to eat is regarded with distaste by some other groups?

Specific dietary requests

Some general guidelines about food and drink follow, but please recall that there is a great deal of variety within every faith. Do not assume that parents of a specific faith will always follow the same pattern – give some time to talk with and listen to individual parents. If you are in any doubt, ask them. Also be ready to talk with the children, as soon as they are old enough to explain to you.

BUDDHISM

This world faith does not have a strict system of beliefs and Buddhists are often expected to reach their own decisions on practical issues such as diet. Many Buddhists decide to be vegetarian, but not all.

CHRISTIANITY

Most Christians do not follow religious rules for their diet, but a few groups do avoid certain foods. Jehovah's Witnesses require that meat has been completely drained of blood and avoid foods like black pudding because of the blood. Mormons avoid black pudding and caffeine in any form, so children should not have cola drinks. Some Rastafarians follow a vegetarian diet close to vegan, avoiding dairy products. If families eat meat, they will probably avoid pork and shellfish. (The Rastafarian faith is a blend of Biblical teachings and African cultural traditions.)

HINDUISM

Some Hindus are vegetarian, but those families who eat meat will avoid beef and beef products in any form, since cows are regarded as sacred and must not be killed. Diary produce is acceptable since the cow does not have to be slaughtered for milk, yogurt or cheese. Watch out for unexpected beef products, for instance, in gelatine used to set puddings. The BSE scare of the 1990s alerted many people to such ingredients and there are alternatives, for instance, a vegetarian form of gelatine.

JUDAISM

The laws of Kashrut (see page 17) determine diet for Jewish families but parents vary in how closely they observe the laws. Orthodox families will be the strictest, but their children will almost certainly attend Jewish nurseries and schools. It is impossible to offer proper Kosher food unless your setting has a kitchen organised along Kosher lines, which means two separate sets of cutlery, crockery and dish washing facilities. The only option for children from an Orthodox family attending a non-Jewish setting will be to bring a packed lunch or snack and their own cutlery. Less strict Jewish families will ask you to ensure that their children are not given pork in any form, nor shellfish.

ISLAM

Muslim families avoid pork in any form. As with meals for Jewish children, you have to watch out for unexpected pork products in processed foods and read the list of ingredients carefully. Any meat or poultry for Muslim children must be from a proper Halal butcher, which will be straightforward if your area has plenty of local Muslim families. If buying Halal meat and poultry is not a practical option, then some families may be content with products from a Kosher butcher (if that is a more practical local alternative). Definitely ask parents about their preference rather than assume. Otherwise, children from Muslim families will need fish or vegetarian meal choices each day.

Sikhism

Some Sikhs are vegetarian, but those who eat meat will probably avoid beef and pork. Families will want meat from a butcher that has definitely *not* been bled in the Halal or Kosher method.

Children's questions

It is worth considering how you will handle children's inquiries about differences in the group. For instance, there will be three broad reasons why children may not be offered a particular food:

- they are allergic to the food
- they really dislike the food
- their family does not eat it on philosophical or religious grounds.

Be honest and straightforward in your explanations, as appropriate to the reason on each occasion. Encourage the children themselves to answer questions if they are confident to do so.

For instance, the question of 'Why won't Aaron eat ham sandwiches?' can be answered with, 'Aaron's family is Jewish and Jewish people believe it is wrong to eat any food that comes from pigs.' If you regularly answer children's questions in a simple and informative way, there may be no further comments, because the group has an understanding that people are just different on some issues. However, replies like, 'Poor Aaron, that's not fair' or 'My Mum says that's silly' can be countered with, 'Most families feel strongly about something and Aaron has plenty of other choices about what he can eat.' Of course, depending on Aaron's age, he may prefer to answer his peers' questions himself and only ask you for help or suggestions in private, if he is stuck for words.

• **To think about** •

Giving thanks for food

A number of world religions have a tradition of giving thanks for food – either at most mealtimes or on special occasions. In your setting you can establish a tradition of giving thanks, but this should be a general appreciation for food and the efforts made in preparation and not a specifically Christian 'saying grace', nor a prayer in any particular faith.

Bear in mind that a repetitive ritual of thanks soon means nothing to children and the aim of this practice is lost in the daily mumble. Instead of giving thanks at each meal or snack, you could encourage the children to make a special thank you to the cook as a person when a favourite pudding has been made. Or you could ensure that children who have made biscuits for tea, or a parent who has sent in some special food, receives a heartfelt thank you from the group, either in words or perhaps a specially completed picture.

Children and traditions of fasting

Giving up specific foods at particular times or fasting for periods is part of religious practice in some faiths and, depending on the timing of the relevant religious celebration, may affect your practice with children.

Periods of fasting or avoiding particular foods used to be common practice within the Christian faith (see page 25). There are a few remaining traditions that you may encounter. Some Christians still avoid meat on Fridays, so children would need an alternative meal without meat. Even if families involve their children in giving up a food for Lent, it is unlikely to be a major ingredient of meals. The possible exception will be if you have families from the Orthodox Christian Church who may follow the tradition of avoiding meat, eggs and milk products for all of Lent.

You are most likely to encounter daytime fasting if you work with children from Muslim families, because they will fast from dawn until sunset during Ramadan (see page 32). Families are careful about bringing children into the tradition over a matter of years and young children are not expected to fast. Older children join the fast for some of the days or for some hours within a day and it is not until puberty that young people become fully part of fasting from food or drink.

If you work in a primary school or an after school club, then you need to respect children's wish to join the fast for short periods of time. Children may be more tired than usual, because they rise with their family to share a pre-dawn meal. Each year Ramadan moves steadily through the seasons and during the summer months a daylight hours fast is long. Children may not want to run around the playground in lively play and will appreciate somewhere to sit peacefully in the shade. Children may also want a quiet room in the school or club for prayer. If you talk with the parents about the children's needs, you will learn more about how you can support the family's faith and show respect.

Clothing and hair

Some faiths have requirements that arise from concerns about modesty linked with religious tradition. Other traditions about hair or clothing have historical reasons linked with the development of a particular faith. For instance:

- Muslim families are likely to be concerned that girls keep their hair and legs covered. The girls may have a scarf worn over the hair or a full head covering which frames the face. Uniform in schools should allow for head covering, perhaps specifying the colour of the material.
- Some Jewish and Christian groups require women and girls to keep their head covered by a scarf, although all the hair may not have to be enclosed.
- Jewish boys from some families will wear a kippa, the skull cap, all the time. Other families will require their sons to wear the kippa only for prayer.
- Rastafarian parents are likely to ask that their daughters keep their hair neatly covered by a scarf and that their sons wear a hat in rasta colours (called a **tam**) which contains their hair. Strict Rastafarians neither cut nor comb their hair, which then twists naturally to form the dreadlocks.
- Sikh males do not have their hair cut and young boys have the hair plaited neatly around their head. When they are older, boys' hair is wound into a jura (a bun) contained by a small cloth covering and teenagers will eventually have a turban.

In any faith some families will be stricter about their children's dress or hair than others, so talk with parents to be guided as to their wishes. Some families may not be very active within the faith, but still follow the general traditions and you should respect their wishes. Problems arise if workers are insensitive to differences between cultural and religious traditions or refuse to take seriously any unfamiliar traditions. Concerns about modesty and undressing for games can be addressed by recognising that many children appreciate some privacy over changing and by discussing some options in what children can wear for dance or games.

Children sometimes wear items that have religious significance. Good practice is to ask the child or parents about the meaning of an item, especially if you have any safety concerns. You should certainly not insist on removing an item from a child just because it looks unimportant to you. Examples include:

- Some children from Christian families may wear a small crucifix on a chain around the neck. Wearing a crucifix is not necessarily a sign of religious commitment; the symbol is often used in secular jewellery.
- Chinese children may wear charms that are associated with good fortune.
- Hindu boys may wear a plaited red and gold bracelet (rakhi) at the festival of Raksha Bandhan (see page 141).
- Sikh children may wear a steel band (Kara) on the right wrist, which is of great importance as one of the five K's, the symbols of the faith worn by Sikhs (see page 50).

Health and hygiene

Good practice will always be to talk with parents about the approach to health in your setting and to understand fully the health needs of individual children. In an emergency you should, of course, call the child's parent, at which point they will take over responsibility for their child. Some families will have specific concerns about treatment that can arise at a time of medical crisis. Jehovah's Witnesses, for instance, are opposed to blood transfusions, but it will be the role of medical staff to deal with the implications of this belief.

Your approach should also encourage children to learn good habits in hygiene. Bear in mind that some religious beliefs include a particular approach to hygiene that should be respected. For instance, Muslim children, and some Sikhs and Hindus, are taught to use the right hand for eating and keep the left for dealing with personal hygiene including toileting. Children are also taught important habits of hand washing before prayer.

9

Overview

Some thoughts on good practice

Children do not develop in a social vacuum. Their experiences are shaped by the environment in which they live and learn and through key adults who bring meaning to children's experiences. There will be many aspects of the lives of children who attend your setting that are the responsibility of their parents. However, you are fully responsible for the way that children are enabled to learn and to think during their time in your setting. The way that you behave will have an impact on the children and your outlook and attitudes will become visible to them through your words and actions.

· *To think about* ·

Good practice will have several strands:

- On one professional level it is important that you understand your obligations within the setting that arise from the policy, the RE syllabus in a school and the background of the law.
- However, on another professional level you are responsible for your own continued learning about world faiths and not only those which are represented in your local area. A positive approach is to extend your knowledge and be willing to learn from all possible sources: not only written material, but also parents and colleagues, local people and not least the children themselves.
- Good practice in this, as in any other

area relevant to children, is that you are prepared to stand back from your own preferred outlook. Be ready to reflect on your own views, whether religious or secular, and be willing to find the common human themes in beliefs and practices, as well as respecting the differences.

- Never lose sight of the children and what they are learning, whether you intend this development or not. It is your role to help the children to develop respect for other people, but within an atmosphere where children feel confident that they too deserve respect.
- It will help if you are honest and straightforward with the children, both in terms of the information that you offer them and over issues for which there is no easy answer.

Responsible workers in early years care and education and in playwork are willing to reflect on their practice and to make changes in how they behave. This book has offered many specific ways to support children's learning and some final ideas follow that can stimulate your own thoughts and those of your team:

- You may have a clear policy of supporting children's spiritual, personal and moral development, but how do you make this happen in practice? What can you see in your setting day by day?
- Are there times when you hear yourself bluntly telling children that they should value something, that one thing is right and another is wrong or that they ought to behave in a particular way? Be honest and not too hard on yourself – everyone at some time says or does something without consideration. Recognise that you have failed to give children reasons and put right your mistake. Telling is rarely as effective as a combination of tell-show-do. How do you, and your team move beyond moral telling?
- How can you ensure a long-term perspective on the children, that they continue to learn step by step? How might you plan in the short, medium and long term in this area? Do you recognise that children will still have a great deal to learn after they have left your setting; it is not your responsibility to try to cover everything.
- In what ways do you work towards realistic expectations for children's understanding, so that you neither overestimate their abilities nor underestimate them?
- In what ways do you show an awareness and respect for children's inner life? How do you ensure that you sometimes take the time to look through their eyes and tune into their concerns and understanding?
- In what ways do you seek to set a good example to children, to be a positive working model of what you mean by abstract ideas like 'respect' or 'consideration'?
- How clear are you about the different options in behaviour for children when you want to avoid negative approaches? Are you clear about what you would like to encourage, as well as what you want to dissuade children from doing?
- Finally, how do you, and your colleagues, remain alert to what the children are actually learning, rather than what you hope they will learn? In what ways do you watch and listen so that you gain a reasonably accurate perspective on what the children have taken away from a visit, a lively period of celebration or a story-telling session?
- What do you learn from the children? What have you wondered about today?

Appendix 1

Further resources

Articles of Faith Ltd, Resource House, Kay Street, Bury BL9 6BU Tel: 0161 763 6232 Fax: 0161 763 5366.
A wide range of artefacts and resources for religious education, CD Roms, books and wall charts and friezes.

Bangladesh Resource and Multi-cultural Book Centre, 1st Floor, 23-25 Hessel Street, London E1 2LR Tel: 0171 488 4243.
Mail-order relevant to a wide range of ethnic groups and religions and a centre that welcomes visitors.

Community Education Development Centre (CEDC), Woodway Park School, Wigston Road, Coventry CV2 2RH Tel 01203 655700.
Projects and publications in the broad area of community education. Practical resources and photo packs.

Community Insight, The Pembroke Centre, Cheney Manor, Swindon SN2 2PQ Tel: 01793 512612.
Mail-order company specialising in publications about children and a range of books for children.

Development Education Centre, 998 Bristol Road, Selly Oak, Birmingham B29 6LE Tel: 0121 472 3255.
Booklets and photo packs on different aspects of development education, families around the world and varied cultures.

Equality Learning Centre, 365 Holloway Road, London N7 6PA Tel: 0171 700 8127.
Resource and information centre for anyone working with under-eights. Publications and workshops, reading and resources lists, posters.

The Festival Shop, 56 Poplar Road, Kings Heath, Birmingham B14 7AG Tel: 0121 444 0444.
Resource books for adults and children, posters and stencils.

Hope Education, Orb Mill, Huddersfield Road, Oldham, Lancashire OL4 2ST Tel: 0161 633 6611.
Resource books, posters and photo packs and religious artefacts.

Letterbox Library, Unit 2D, Leroy House, 436 Essex Road, London N1 3QP Tel: 0171 226 1633.
Mail-order children's books, specialising in a multicultural list.

National Early Years Network, 77 Holloway Road, London N7 8JZ
Tel: 0171 607 9573.
NEYN publishes a yearly wall chart with the major religious festivals and posters of children of different ethnic background.

NES Arnold Ltd, Ludlow Hill Road, West Bridgford, Nottingham
NG2 6HD Tel: 0115 971 7700.
NES Arnold publish a range of festival packs including information and suggested activities.

Pre-school Learning Alliance (through PPA Promotion), 45-49 Union Road, Croydon CR0 2XU Tel: 0181 684 9542.
They produce booklets and a set of festival friezes.

Religion in Evidence are part of Technology Teaching Systems Ltd at Monk Road, Alfreton, Derbyshire DE55 7RL Tel: 01773 830255.
They produce a wide range of materials for school age children, including religious artefacts.

Save the Children, 17 Grove Lane, London SE5 8RD Tel: 0171 703 5400.
A good source for booklets, photo packs and other visual materials.

Shap Working Party on World Religions in Education, 36 Causton Street, London SW1P 4AU Tel: 0171 932 1194.
Produces a yearly calendar of religious festivals combined with an informative booklet. The journal *World religions in education* is published each year and takes a theme within RE. The Working Party shares premises with the National Society's Religious Education Centre, a resource and advice centre that welcomes visitors and enquiries by letter or telephone (same number as above).

Step by Step Ltd, Holgate Street, Waterhead, Oldham, Lancs OL4 2JF
Tel: 0845 3001089.
Materials for children to use in celebration of festivals, relevant craft materials for displays and making cards, dressing up clothes to cover a range of ethnic groups, pictures, jigsaws and books.

Tamarind Ltd, PO Box 296, Camberley, Surrey GU15 1QW
Tel: 01276 683979.
A wide range of books, puzzles and posters that show children of different ethnic backgrounds.

Unicef, 55-56 Lincoln's Inn Fields, London WC2A 3NB
Tel: 0171 405 5592.
Their calendars and diaries, like those for most of the major children's

charities, include the main religious celebrations for the year. They are also a good source of pictures of children from around the world, in postcards or the illustrations of diaries and calendars.

Westhill RE Centre, Westhill College, Selly Oak, Birmingham B29 6LL
Tel: 0121 472 7248 Fax: 0121 415 5399.
The centre offers information and advice about RE. They also publish books and booklets, photopacks and videos.

Appendix 2

Links to qualifications

This book will directly support you in your study for the following qualifications:

- The BTEC National in Childhood Studies (Nursery Nursing) which has a core module (number 6251K) titled *Modern beliefs and religions.*
- The levels 2 and 3 NVQ/SVQs in Early Years Care and Education and the NVQ/SVQs in Playwork do not have separate units on religion. However, the qualifications are all underpinned by an emphasis on equal opportunities and anti-discriminatory practice, which includes religious and cultural background.
- The modules on equal opportunities and anti-discriminatory practice in the CACHE training programmes all mention religion within this topic. The specific modules are module 1 in the Certificate in Child Care and Education, module C in the Diploma in Nursery Nursing and module 10 in the Advanced Diploma in Child Care and Education. Many of the other modules mention religious belief or practice in the context of good practice in the care of children, in developing a well-rounded curriculum and in partnership with parents.

Index

Age of Aquarius 65–7
agnostic 60
artefacts 164–5
assembly, school 60, 124
astrology 8, 65–7, 72, 88, 129, 147
atheist 60
awe and wonder 90–2, 115, 161

Baisakhi 50, 54, 148–9
books, use of 128, 153–4, 155–160
Buddha, the 42–5, 128
Buddhism 4, 40, 41–8, 57, 58, 67, 100,
    145–8, 164, 173

caste 37, 40
Catholic 4, 25, 164
celebrations (see festivals)
Celtic revival 68–70, 73
Children Act 1989 107–111, 112
Children Act (Scotland) 1995 111, 112
Children (Northern Ireland) Order 1995 111
Chinese New Year 72, 147–8, 151
Christianity 5–7, 17–26, 57, 58, 60, 65, 68,
    86, 95, 100, 129–134, 173, 175
Christmas 7, 24, 120, 125, 126
church schools 101–2
clothing 17, 33, 41, 48, 55, 152, 163, 176
collective worship 99, 102, 106, 107, 113
conversations with,
    children 77–8, 79–80, 94, 156, 174
    colleagues vi, 96, 121, 126, 172, 178
    parents 96, 120, 124–5, 178
craft activities 127–8, 169
cultural tradition vi, 5–6, 22, 23, 85–6, 115

denominational schools 101–2
design 169
desirable learning outcomes (see early learning
    goals)
Divali 10, 40, 54, 125, 142–5, 149
Druidery 69

Easter 7, 24, 132–4
early learning goals 88, 103–4
Education Acts in,
    England and Wales 98–105
    Northern Ireland 106
    Scotland 105
ethnic group 109, 112, 118, 170
existentialism 61–4, 73

faith stories 155–8
fasting 25, 29, 32, 133, 167, 175–6
Father Christmas 78, 127, 131
festivals 15–16, 24–5, 31–2, 48, 54, 57, 70,
    114, 116, chapter 7
food and drink 5, 17, 25, 32–3, 48, 55, 152,
    171–5
funerals 15, 23, 31, 38, 41, 47, 53, 61

geography 170
guilt 85, 86
Guru Gobind Singh 51, 53, 55, 149
Guru Granth Sahib 37, 51, 54, 148
Guru Nanak 48, 54, 149, 150

hair 55, 176
Hanukkah 10, 16, 136–7
harvest festivals 24, 134
Hijrah 26, 31, 137–8
Hinduism 34–41, 44, 49, 57, 58, 67, 100,
    140–5, 178
history 169–170
Holi 39, 54, 140–1
holy books 12, 19–20, 28, 36, 44–5, 51, 58
human needs and faith 1–3, 73
Humanism vi, 9, 59–61, 73, 81, 110, 125
hygiene 41, 55, 177–8

Id-ul-Adha 32, 139–40
Id-ul-Fitr 32, 138–9
initiation ceremonies 14, 23, 30, 37–8, 47, 50,
    53, 95
inspection 102, 108, 113

Islam   26–33, 57, 58, 100, 137–140, 170, 173, 175

Jehovah's Witnesses   20, 125, 177
Jesus Christ   17–21, 27, 66, 68, 77, 86, 128, 129
Judaism   11–17, 57, 58, 65, 100, 134–7, 173

Kathina Day   48, 146
Ks, five of Sikhism   50, 177
Kwanzaa   127

language and communication   77–80, 165–6
Lent   24, 33, 133, 167
Locally Agreed Syllabus   100–1
lunar calendar   8, 31, 137, 147

mathematics   167
mediation   83–3, 96
meditation   45, 67, 164
moral development   81–8, 166–7
moral values   60, 81, 83, 116, 151
Mothering Sunday   134
Muhammad, the Prophet S.A.W.   26–29, 137
music   169
Muslim (see Islam)
myths and legends   155, 158–9

naming ceremonies   5, 14, 23, 30, 37, 47, 61
natural world   70–1, 74, 91, 115
New Age movements   vi, 8, 64–74, 110
New Testament   18, 20, 86
New Year celebrations   16, 31, 40, 72, 147–8, 151
Noble Eightfold Path   43–4, 45
Northern Ireland,
   early years and playwork   111
   education   5, 106–7, 112
nursery education   104, 106
nursery nurses in schools   104–5, 122

Old Testament   12, 19, 20, 27, 32, 139
Orthodox Church   4, 24, 129, 132, 175

paranormal   71–2
partnership with parents   119–120, 124–5
Pentecostal   24, 160
personal care   120, 170–1
personal identity   94–5, 120
Pesach   15, 18, 135, 164
pilgrimage   25–6, 40, 55, 57, 67, 152
places of worship   12–13, 21, 37, 45, 51, 55, 161–3

policy   113–116, 120, 122, 178, 179
political movements   2–3
prayer   74, 176, 177 (see also worship)
prosocial behaviour   82–5
Protestant   3, 4
Purim   15, 134–5

Qur'an   26, 32, 58, 95

Race Relations Act 1976   111, 121
Raksha Bandhan   39, 141–2, 177
Rama   35, 143
Ramayana   36, 143
Rastafarians   100, 160, 176
registration   61, 108–111
religious affiliation of settings   101–2, 119–120
religious education (RE)   98–107
religious instruction   30, 93, 95, 98, 125
respect   vii, 10, 80, 104, 116–7, 123, 125, 126, 162–3, 178
Rosh Hashanah   16

science   7, 167–8
Scotland,
   early years and playwork   111, 112
   education   105–6, 122
secularisation   6–8
Shabbat   13–15
Sikhism   40, 48–56, 57, 58, 100, 148–150, 174
Solar calendars   8
spiritual development   64, 67, 88–90
spirituality   88–96
story-telling   128, 153, 155–7
symbols in religions   16, 22, 29–30, 38–9, 46, 52, 67, 162

Torah   11, 12, 32, 39, 95

uncompromising beliefs   110, 117
Unitarian Church   68
UN Convention on the Rights of the Child   112, 122

Vishnu   35, 143
visits to place of worship   161–3

weddings   14, 23, 30–1, 38, 47, 53, 61
Wesak   48, 145–6
Wicca   69
worship   13, 21, 37, 45, 51

Yom Kippur   16